W9-DEU-169

INTERIOR DIVINE:

Walking You Through the Transformation of Your Home

INTERIOR DIVINE:

Walking You Through the Transformation of Your Home

By Jayne M. Pelosi

Photographic contributions by Kelli Ruggere

Boston

Interior Divine:
Walking You Through the Transformation of Your Home

By Jayne M. Pelosi
Photographic contributions by Kelli Ruggere

Photos pages 7, 19, 25, 29, 34, 43, 51, 65, 73, 85, 107, 111, 118, 121, 125, 126, 127, 135, 138, 152, 153, 167 ©
        2005 JupiterImages Corporation
Photos pages 17, 27, 30, 35, 45, 59, 60, 61, 66, 72, 76, 78, 81, 96, 99, 110, 117, 122, 123, 129, 133, 137, 139, 151,
        155, 159, 161 © 2005 Elizabeth Nollner
Photos page 55 © 2005 Phillip Nollner
Photo page 37 © 1998 Denise Passaretti
Photos pages 77, 84, 137, 150, 154, 169 © 1992-2005 Jayne Pelosi
Photos pages 12, 44, 75, 79, 82, 83, 91, 142, 165, 166 © 1992-1996 Charles Reeves
Photos pages 9, 11, 21, 22, 26, 31, 36, 39, 47, 48, 49, 54, 56, 63, 64, 67, 68, 71, 74, 76, 77, 80, 86, 87, 88, 89, 93,
        94, 95, 98, 99, 100, 102, 104, 106, 113, 114, 116, 123, 128, 129, 130, 131, 132, 134, 141, 143, 145, 146,
        156, 157, 160, 162, 164, 168, 170, 171, 197 © 1997-2005 Kelli Ruggere
Photo page 196 © 2001 Gretje Ferguson
Illustrations pages 15, 23, 24, 25, 33, 52, 53, 57, 70, 109, 115, 136 © 2005 Jayne Pelosi

Published by Acanthus Publishing
343 Commercial Street
Unit 214, Union Wharf
Boston, MA 02109

Publisher's Cataloging-In-Publication Data
(Prepared by The Donohue Group, Inc.)

Pelosi, Jayne M., 1959-
   Interior divine : walking you through the transformation of your home / by Jayne M. Pelosi ; photographic contributions
by Kelli Ruggere.

   p. : ill. ; cm.
   Includes bibliographical references and index.
   ISBN-13: 978-0-9754810-8-0
   ISBN-10: 0-9754810-8-8

1. Interior decoration--Handbooks, manuals, etc. 2. Interior decoration--Planning--Handbooks, manuals, etc. I.
Ruggere, Kelli. II. Title.

NK2115 .P45 2005
747

All rights reserved. No part of this book may be reproduced or transmitted in any form or by any means, electronic
or mechanical, including photocopying, recording or by any information storage and retrieval system, without written
permission from the author, except for the inclusion of brief quotations in a review.

Copyright © 2005, Jayne M. Pelosi

Design and Layout: Anthony Manes
Illustrations: Anthony Manes
Editorial: Elizabeth Nollner
Cover Photography: Kelli Ruggere, Elizabeth Nollner, Gretje Ferguson

Printed in the United States of America

To my husband and soul mate, Steven —
whenever I see your face, I know I'm home.

TABLE OF CONTENTS

PREFACE

I have always considered myself a natural teacher. Even though studying education at Boston University for one semester taught me I had no desire to be in a classroom, it did reinforce something I was beginning to understand about myself at the tender age of eighteen. And that was that I had a strong need to influence and inspire others. Whether it was sharing a strong political belief with willing ears, or simply sharing a well-loved family recipe, I had no desire to keep my ideas to myself. Let me offer this apologia here and now to the countless souls I may have offended over the years: I just couldn't help myself. I know now at the tender age of forty-something that we all have gifts and none of us are meant to keep them to ourselves. I would like to think that now I'm better at sharing only with those who choose to receive. So this, my first book, is all about sharing with you my wit and wisdom of being an interior designer for these past twelve years, written from the perspective of a teacher, or a design mentor if you will.

I came into the fanciful and abundant field of interior design in a circuitous manner. Having studied psychology in college, I spent a few years working as a counselor in a psychiatric ward of a general hospital. When I realized I didn't have the temperament to deal with chronically ill patients, I shifted gears to a place that allowed me to use my people skills in a different way: I found myself in the corporate world in the sales department. Being a salesperson eventually led to becoming a sales manager, which ultimately led to my running a $2.3 million branch in the telecommunications industry as a branch manager. What does all of this have to do with interior design you might ask? Much more than you might think.

As a salesperson, the ability to truly listen to a prospect was always one of my natural instincts. The sales trade used to say, "Find their hot button and go in for the close." I preferred to think I was empathetically hearing their concerns and finding perfect solutions. Then as a manager, it was all about cultivating someone's gifts through training and endless teaching. And the best teachers on earth know the secret to producing successful students: never stop asking questions. You ask and explore until you fully expose the root of their misunderstanding; only then can you provide them with the tools they need to succeed for themselves. Whether I was providing feedback on someone's sales techniques or offering decorative solutions for a client's interiors as I do today, I have always found it highly rewarding creating a silk purse from a sow's ear.

So while I was enjoying a fulfilling career in the corporate world, back home we were busily renovating a fixer-upper Victorian gem we had just bought.

Decorating has always been a passion of mine, even as a child, but I never saw myself as talented enough to do it professionally, so it remained a hobby. But when my home project was complete, friends would stream in and consistently ask my then-husband who we used to decorate the place. "Well, Jayne did it," he would answer and mouths would drop and eyebrows would rise. The seed was planted then and there. This was 1988.

I continued to decorate my own home and the homes of close friends for several years. I recall wanting to do over the sitting room one year after we had already "redone" it, and my first husband getting annoyed, wondering how many times we were going to redecorate the newly redecorated house. I distinctly remember the sad moment when I cancelled all of my interior design magazine subscriptions because they were just too much of a tantalizing lure. Pages and pages of glossy colorful images beckoning me into a world of gorgeous possibility were too hard to resist.

It wasn't until my first marriage ended that I made the first bold move toward my heart's desire: I started Renaissance Interior Design on a part-time basis, hoping someday to make it my full-time career. This was 1993.

Then, when the company for whom I was working was acquired by a large corporation whose core values conflicted with my own, it was time to make the leap. I went on my own in May 1996 and have never looked back. People often ask me what motivated me to make such a 180-degree shift in careers. I tell them that making the transition from branch manger to interior design entrepreneur was almost seamless. In my mind, the job descriptions were more similar than one would think: listening, problem solving, managing people and deadlines, and executing creative solutions. This new job, however, had one huge extra benefit: I was my own boss.

Let me digress for a moment. I recently read an article in an interior design magazine about *good* interior design. When shopping for a *good* interior designer, the author maintained that one should never consider hiring someone unless she or he had a background in fine art, art history, or architecture. I laughed out loud. "How near-sighted," I thought to myself, "and how sadly misguided." Without a doubt, these disciplines offer substantial content and perspective to a designer. But the author seemed to have missed a very important part of what it means to be a good interior designer, and that has to do with people. It also has to do with soul. Specifically, does the designer have one? And are they able to touch the souls of their clients so that they can truly design for the client, and not their own portfolios? Or more generally, are they able to motivate, inspire, teach, and reach their audience, so in some small way they have changed their lives? Too over the top? How about aiming for leaving people happier and richer for having known you?

Or as the Buddhists say, "Leave a small wake when you pass."

What I find particularly amusing is that for interior designers, it's now considered very in vogue to have a background in psychology. Recently I read an article in *The Wall Street Journal* about the newest trend in interior design: hiring a design therapist. They advocate finding a professional who has the ability to truly listen and ask probing questions about your habits and lifestyle, and especially, to have the ability to negotiate the contrasting opinions of most couples. Ah, the satisfaction of being a trendsetter, or at least having been ahead of the curve!

For the past twelve years, I have had the privilege of working with hundreds of fascinating clients. Many were families with pets and children, a few were newly-divorced men eager to discover their design identity apart from the influence of their wives. Some were career women, some were empty nesters. All provided me with invaluable lessons. And many provided the fodder for this book. My clients tell me repeatedly that not only did I leave their rooms looking better than when I initially walked in, but that I taught them something. I taught them to listen to their hearts and, just as important, to listen to what their spouses were trying to communicate. I mediated many a quarreling couple at odds with each other's design plan. I've taught, and continue to teach, my clients how to express their highest and most fulfilled self in their homes, not terribly unlike what I taught my sales reps way back in the corporate world. Most important for the purpose of this book, I found areas people tend to get stuck in the design process.

This is not an A-Z encyclopedia on interior design. It's not a retrospective of design styles from the 1700s to the present day. And this definitely is not written by an architect, art historian, or fine artist. It's a practical and straightforward primer that identifies what I consider to be simple ways to improve your home, and therefore enhance your life. It's my hope that even the most overwhelmed and unhappy dwellers will pick up this book and begin to find relief. It's written so that if you decide to implement only one or two ideas, your home can be transformed. And it's my experience that when you begin to transform someone's home and how they feel inside it, you begin to transform their lives.

Jayne Pelosi
September 2005
Duxbury, MA

INTERIOR
DIVINE

Many years ago when a friend first suggested I write a book, my first response was "Who the heck would read it?" followed by "What could I possibly say that hasn't been said a million times?" Happily, twelve years later, I'm writing in a time when the field of interior design and home crafting is incredibly popular, enjoying wildly successful public appeal. From time to time, when large corporations in the home care field are developing new products, they invite me to come and speak. I enthusiastically tell them all about the latest trends in both style and materials, as well as advise them as to what improvements they could make in the home care products they currently manufacture, based on my own and my clients' experiences. I tell these corporate clients that not since the fifties has the field of interior design and all of its adjunct industries enjoyed such attention and prosperity.

The fact that women are focusing on their homes again is very good news to these corporations. And readers: This is very good news for you too! Yes, I know you may be stuck in your design process, but imagine if it was 1980! Your options would be far more limited; there would be no HGTV, no Internet. Your neighbors might even berate you for daring to think about your interiors. There were far greater fish to fry: You (my female readers) would be expected to don a lace bow tie around your neck, put on your power suit, and compete in the highly-coveted corporate world.

So here we all are, some twenty-five years later, with renewed interest in our homes. Perhaps you remember that author and future-trend predictor Faith Popcorn first coined the expression "cocooning" in her 1991 best-seller *The Popcorn Report*. She predicted that due to a variety of circumstances – including a backlash from what has been called the "decade of conspicuous consumption," and the subsequent stock market crash in 1987 – Americans would be hunkering down, moving inside their homes, and nesting. And guess what? We've been nesting steadily since the early nineties, which has given rise to literally hundreds of cottage industries all serving the interior design field, such as aromatherapy, personal organizers (and all of their products/tools), and mass-produced slipcovers, just to name a few. This is why today, more than any time in recent history, you have a plethora of wonderful options, styles, and choices for your design project.

However, I know having thousands of choices doesn't necessarily make deciding any easier – in fact, in some ways it can make it worse. I'm often told by my clients that starting a design project can be overwhelming at best, and more often agonizing to the point that they would rather put it off indefinitely and live in chaos. I have met countless clients who have confessed to living in their homes for years before they put up a single curtain. And others who avoid certain rooms in their homes entirely because they can't make them "work" and would rather avoid the pain of sitting in them. I feel sad when my female clients tell me they are embarrassed that they can't pull their homes together beautifully on their own and need to hire an interior designer; as if it should be a genetic predisposition that comes with being female. I make light of their remark by telling them two things: (1) I break out in a cold sweat whenever I walk into a computer store, much like they do in a fabric store. And (2) if every woman was a natural-born designer, I would still be managing sales reps in the telecommunications industry. That usually makes them feel better. Basically, if you share any of these sentiments with my clients, this book is for you.

Or maybe you're not in design turmoil. Maybe you have a good handle on what you want your home to look like and you're just looking for fresh ideas. I would love to think my book helped you do-it-yourselfers take your interiors to the next fabulous level. Who knows, you might get really inspired and decide to quit your day job and pursue your heart's desire as an interior designer! The more the merrier I say!

However you feel about decorating, this book is about those chronic areas where, time and again, people get stuck in the design process. I offer ways to think about and prioritize these often frustrating and stress-inducing decisions. Usually the "I'm stuck" place is at the very beginning – not knowing what decision to make first, what item to purchase first, "What the heck is my style anyway?" Perhaps it's my background in psychology, or the fact that I enjoy teaching, but when friends began asking me "What is your book about?" I replied, "I like to think of it as a primer, written from the perspective of a very spiritual, yet pragmatic, design therapist who happened to throw in a few decorating tricks of the trade here and there." I think that's unique. I don't think decorating advice has ever been packaged quite that way before. At least not a million times.

While I would love to have the pleasure of being in all of your homes walking you through the transformative process of upgrading, uplifting, or defining your interiors, sadly I cannot. Instead I wrote this book so you can begin this process on your own, but with me as your design mentor.

I don't preach about which styles are better than others. I firmly believe everyone has his or her own unique design personality; you just may not have met it yet. My hope is that once you've finished the book, you'll have been introduced to this wonderful spirit and will choose to honor it by beginning your own design transformation. Don't be scared! Maybe all you'll choose to do is lower your artwork and pull in your furnishings. But if that's all it takes to bring you a greater sense of balance and comfort in your space, then I have been successful. *Andiamo!*

Part I:
Know Your Basics

"I have a lot of good design ideas; I just don't know where to start." This is what I often hear when I begin relationships with my clients. As obvious as it may seem, a fair amount of thinking and planning should be the very first steps to a design process. And if you live with a significant other, sitting down over a glass of wine or hot cup of tea and having a quiet conversation about your ideas is also a necessary first step. You may be amazed and pleasantly surprised at what the other person has in mind.

The decorating process begins by developing a foundation on which you can build your plan, whether you're just refreshing one room or about to undertake a large design project. Some of the following ideas are broad in scope, such as how to get inspired and discovering what makes you feel great in a room. Others are very specific, such as my suggestions for your "To Do" list when you actually start spending money.

Several of these topics, such as those regarding color, pattern, and balance, were written with particular clients in mind, all of whom had worked with other designers in the past. These clients all voiced a similar sentiment, which, if I can summarize, was essentially, "No other designer has taken the time to really teach me about my options. They make recommendations based on trends, not on what my facial expressions are telling them." These topics seem to regularly get an "Ah-ha, now I get it!" from clients, and that's very gratifying to this teacher/design mentor. I hope you'll find them as eye-opening as my clients have. So let's begin!

Chapter One
Getting Started

Where Should We Begin?

Clients often ask me what the ideal sequence of events should be when starting a decorating project. "Where do we begin; should we start with the rug?
Or should we pick out paint first and work from that point?" Whether you're
starting from scratch, that is, replacing all the contents of a room, or just
integrating a few new additions to an existing arrangement, there's an order I
recommend that makes the project not only easier, but allows for the greatest
options and flexibility.

Please note that this is the sequence I recommend for *choosing* these elements, not necessarily installing them. Most contractors would opt to paint
walls before a new carpet is installed, but for the purpose of deciding on
selections, my recommended sequence is as follows:

1. Pick your area rug first, if you want a patterned or Oriental rug, because
there are more limited choices in area rugs than fabrics; you'll have a better chance of coordinating fabric to your patterned rug than the other way
around. Once you do find an area rug that you like, you can then translate
its colors into other elements in your room, such as paint and accessories.

If you'll be going with plain wall-to-wall carpet, e.g. broadloom, where a
myriad of colors exist, you don't need to make this your first step. You can
choose the rug once other decorative decisions have been made. Same
rule exists for hard flooring. So many options exist in hardwood, laminate,
and tile flooring that you can make this decision once your other decorative
choices have been made. You should be able to easily find flooring that
enhances the other design choices you've made in the space towards the
end of your project.

2. Pick your upholstered furnishings next. This applies when decorating
a living room or great room/den. Many clients feel safer choosing a solid
color fabric for the largest piece of furniture (sofa or sectional) and bringing
in pattern on the side chairs. Other clients choose to make a bold statement
with a patterned sofa and balancing that with solid side pieces. This is a
personal choice; just make sure you really love the bold pattern enough to
be looking at an expanse of eight to twelve yards of it, should you place it on
the sofa. When decorating a bedroom or dining room, where wood may be
the predominant element, choose your wood tones now as well.

3. Select your fabrics for the room. This is usually in respect to window treatments. Some clients adore long flowing drapery panels; others prefer tailored top treatments, e.g. valances. But because there are literally thousands of fabric patterns from which to choose, you should have *no* trouble finding a fabric that speaks to you. Your budget may determine whether you purchase store-bought items or can splurge on custom treatments. There is more on both fabric selection and window treatments further along in the book.

4. Choose the color of your paint last, well almost last, just before you pick out the accessories. This is where a lot of clients get confused. I have been brought into many homes where the clients have already committed to a new paint color, then have a great deal of trouble "backing into" the fabric selection. It can be done, but depending on the new shade that's just been put on the walls, you may have a harder time finding just the right color match in your fabrics. It's much easier to go the other way and match a paint color to fabric; indeed many paint stores will be able to duplicate a color directly from your fabric samples.

Interestingly, the area rug was added last to this eclectic salon. I wanted the rug to add a jolt of pattern to rescue the room from looking too staid or serious.

Special note: If you prefer wallpaper to paint, there are two ways to approach this decision. If you plan to choose wallpaper with a dominant pattern, pick out your wallpaper *before* you choose the fabrics for the room. If, on the other hand, you tend to favor subtle or more neutral wallpapers, you can select it *after* you've selected your fabrics. The trick is deciding which element will be the "main player" and which element will be the "supporting actor," if you will, in your design theme. In the photo to the right, the clients really wanted a stunning patterned wallpaper to set the décor theme and thus be the main pattern in the room. The window treatments in this case became the secondary focus and were intentionally made in a solid, more subdued fabric.

5. Finally, you'll want to apply the icing on the cake, which includes all of the wonderful accessories with which you choose to fill and finish the space, such as artwork, pillows, vases and plants, candles, statues, and trinkets.

Having said *all* of that... That's not to say that you can't pick up a specialty piece here or there, out of sequence, if you will. You may find an unusual piece of furniture or special work of art that you know you *have* to have in your newly decorated space. Or perhaps you've inherited a sentimental family heirloom that you'd like to incorporate in the room. I highly encourage such activity; this is what truly personalizes our interiors. If you find yourself, in fact, having just such an inspiration piece as your decorative springboard, go forth and create the room around this muse.

In this dramatic formal dining room, the wallpaper was the star of the show. We chose it first, and then selected both the fabric for the chairs and the window treatments based on the tones in the wallpaper.

Inspiration Can Come From Anything, Anywhere

In my twelve years as an interior designer, the following scenario has happened more times than I can count on two hands: A client comes back from, say, a vacation at a charming B&B in Vermont and exclaims, "I changed my mind – I no longer want to do the bedroom in the contemporary look, I want to do it country cottage!" Or, a newly married couple back from the Yucatan has desperate décor cravings of clay pottery and vividly colored serapes. These desires are perfectly natural; we all want to surround ourselves with things that evoke beautiful or exciting memories. Can we incorporate such objects into our everyday décor? Absolutely.

The ethnic fabric wall hanging above the couch served as the inspiration for this Jamaican bachelor's den.

The reality is that inspiration comes from anywhere and everywhere. You never know when you're going to be moved by a pillow, wall color, or a combination of rich hues found in a floral arrangement. Because one-hundred percent of my clients are neither artists nor designers, they tend to ignore those moments when their senses say "Whoa, that's gorgeous." Or when they're in a room and viscerally feel calm or excited or just very happy. I invite you to pay attention to those moments, especially if you're considering taking on a design project.

If the thought of starting a design project makes you break out in a sweat, *but* the prospect of living in *that* room makes you feel even worse, take heart. There's a series of small steps you can take to begin the process and make the overall job easier and more manageable:

1. Seriously look at the room and ask yourself of all its existing elements:

"Do I love or at least like this piece?" If the answer is a resounding *"No,"* it's time to donate it to charity, lovingly give it to a friend, or gently add it to the trash pile. In a soulfully decorated room, where you're true to yourself and your family, there's no room for "maybes." To quote one of my favorite personal coaches, Cheryl Richardson, the choices you make must be on your "absolute *yes*" list or it won't work.

2. Now that you've emptied the room of the pieces that don't belong (and this includes pieces from a past marriage or a past difficult relationship that don't bring you good memories when you look at them) ask yourself, "What would I put on my wish list?" Perhaps a plush comfy chair for reading and journal writing? Perhaps attractive and functional storage units for all that clutter? Perhaps the artwork you did as a budding five-year-old artist that's begging to be framed and honored on your walls?

To make things concrete, consider writing down four or five adjectives or phrases that describe your current space, and on the other side of the page, write down four or five adjectives that you *wish* described the space. Here's an example:

My living/dining room area is:
- Too pale in color
- Very elegant but a little stuffy
- Filled with expensive pieces
- A little "cold" feeling

I want to:
- Add more color
- Give it a slightly funky, "edgy" feel
- Make it feel warmer, more inviting
- Have it relate or connect somehow to my adjacent kitchen

I was just in a space with a new client who felt exactly this way about her combination living and dining room. The room in many ways was breathtaking; I know she spent a great deal of money to decorate it, yet she wasn't fully happy with the outcome. So here's what we did:

- Painted the walls in her adjacent kitchen a rich deep plum.

- Added plum and black velvet pillows to her elegant ivory living room sofas.

- For added warmth, we added two deep-hued area rugs: one for under the dining room table and the other for the living room sitting area. To obtain that "edgy" feel she wanted, we made one a leopard area rug and the other a slightly contemporary rug with deep plum, caramel, and black tones.

- Switched one of her conservative gilded mirrors with a leopard frame mirror she had in another room.

- Removed the dead dried hydrangeas in a wreath that hung over the fireplace and substituted with deep plum silk stems; this totally freshened the wreath.

• Substituted many of her ivory pillar candles for plum and deep lilac candles; this not only emphasized the new accent color in the living/dining room areas but related both of these rooms to the adjacent kitchen, which had been totally white and begging for color.

You get the idea? Sometimes all it takes is articulating your complaints and writing down your wish list, then, budget allowing, tackling the corrections.

3. Now for the fun part – getting inspired. Start paying attention to places you visit. Notice how restaurants are decorated. Observe (without making them nervous) how others decorate their homes. Notice anything and everything visual that makes you feel good. I once designed a powder room around a T-shirt, no joke. My client fell in love with the combination of colors and voilà, her powder room was bathed in Biminy blue walls, creamy white wainscoting, and zebra-patterned drapes with black rugs and linens. I also vividly remember a few years ago a couple telling me, "We want a sofa like they have on the television show *Mad About You*." Does anyone remember it? It was a plush and comfy sofa that featured several prints and patterns of fabric – very homey!

You see? Inspiration can be found anywhere. As the Buddhists say, "When the student is ready, the teacher appears." It's no different in home design; when you're open to something, in this case open to inspiration, I promise it will come to you. It's time to relish in the abundance and partake in the feast.

Create A Decorating Kit For Your Projects

Even if you're just beginning a project, and are in the inspiration stage, commit to staying organized with all of your visual aids. For instance, I always carry any inspiration pieces I'm designing a room around – like the T-shirt for the room I just mentioned – until all the design elements have been selected.

It could be a scarf, a small piece of blown glass, or a photo of the Alaskan tundra. Whatever visual stimulus strikes you as something you want to see translated into a space, make sure you always have it with you in a small bag or satchel. I'm a big fan of the large plastic bags that have the "zipper seal" built in. I'm a bigger fan of collecting the heavier plastic bags that store-bought linens (pillowcases, drapery panels, etc.) come in. Some come with zippers, others snap shut. (After dropping a manila envelope in a big muddy puddle, I immediately switched to plastic.) All of these will protect your visual cues while allowing you to see the contents clearly when shopping.

Along with a file folder for each client, I regularly carry around with me one of those plastic bags to hold any three-dimensional items. In it you'll often find any and all of the following goodies:

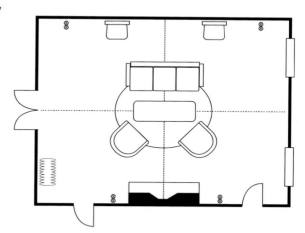

- Paint chips
- Fabric swatches and trim samples
- Photos and magazine tear sheets
- Wallpaper swatches
- Arm covers from chairs to match fabrics
- Pillowcases
- Granite and tile pieces

And never to be forgotten, accurate measurements for all spaces to be filled. Make sure you measure all aspects of your space, including

Your sketches don't have to be this professional looking! Just make sure you include all important dimensions and features, including where outlets, phone jacks, and pesky things like radiators are located.

wall lengths and heights, unbroken wall spans (no windows or other elements in the way), and even areas of surfaces you're trying to fill, such as a sideboard you'd like some accessories for. Consider sketching a plan of your room using all your measurements and marking all the existing furniture and artwork and any built-in elements, such as windows, and even outlets so you know where things can be placed that need electricity. The more detailed information you have, the more likely you are to buy items for your room that fit perfectly to the space. There's nothing more frustrating than buying a ninety-four-inch sofa for what turns out to be an eighty-eight-inch wall.

If you would like some help recording your measurements, you can photo-copy the measurements chart in the Appendix and fill in all your information. Now you have a complete and portable guide to your available space!

While you may not be able to fit this kit in your daily satchel or handbag, I recommend keeping it readily available in your car. It's very likely that in your travels, you'll unexpectedly happen by a store or showroom that looks inviting. Having all your supplies and information handy will ensure that you'll never miss an opportunity to make an all-important design decision when it presents itself. And the Universe being what it is, once you've committed to upgrading your home even in some small way, you can count on those situations presenting themselves. Here's to serendipity!

The First Step To A Beautiful Interior: Declutter!

Nothing is more unsettling and disruptive than piles and piles of clutter. Clutter is not only visually unappealing but it drains us of our vital energy – energy better spent on working, playing, and nurturing our relationships. It's impossible, and actually irrelevant, to spend time and money decorating a room if you haven't begun tackling the clutter. There are hundreds of good books on organizing, not to mention websites devoted to the topic, so there are plenty of specialized resources to consult. If you feel your clutter is more than you can tackle on our own, consider contacting the National Association of Professional Organizers (NAPO) so you can find a professional in your area.

If you think you can pick away at your excess belongings without help, here's an easy strategy that, once adopted, will keep you streamlined for life – the C.A.R.D. rule. Everything you own should fall into one of four categories:

• Current (which means you use it regularly)
• Archival (important but doesn't need to be in your day-to-day living space)
• Rubbish
• Donate

Some of my clients begin with their clothes, others begin with their household accessories and trinkets, and then again, others start small with just a junk drawer. I once emptied a junk drawer of my own that had become out of control. I wanted to purge the stuff, but what if I needed those three eyeglass repair kits one day? I promised myself that I would put all of the contents in a clear plastic box and store it in the basement, and if in *one* year I never went back to the box in search of something, I vowed I would get rid of everything in it. Only once during the course of the year did I go back to the box, looking for, of all things, an electric lint buzzer (the little razor that buzzes off pills on your knit sweaters). Everything else in that junk box was useless to me, so I followed through on my promise to myself and either threw out or donated all the other contents to the local "swap" station at our town dump. It helped to not have to decide right away, but you need to give yourself a statute of limitations on procrastination! Date the box and stick to your goal. It was actually revealing to see that I tend to collect and keep more than I really need.

Ideally, tackle those piles of paper, clothing, kids' projects, past tax returns

– anything that's routinely found in mounds on floors and surfaces – and start today. In all of your closets, keep an empty bin so you can get in the regular habit of dropping in charitable items – make it easy and make it effortless. My experience is that if you begin the process of streamlining, one pile at a time, you'll feel lighter. You'll also feel kind and generous, especially if your charitable category is big! And you'll have set the stage for your gorgeous new interior.

In an uncluttered space, good design can simply mean the careful placement of a mid-century modern side chair and a hand-painted oil hung above it. Let the pieces speak for themselves.

Chapter Two
Color and Pattern

How Much Color Would *You* Like?

Many years ago, I worked with a client who was committed to adding color to her life. She was newly divorced from a spouse who, for his own reasons, craved the peace and serenity of beige – everywhere, that is. She had color ideas for every room of her new abode and wanted to begin by bathing all of the walls in deep, rich hues.

Now, most people who know me would agree that I'm a huge enthusiast of color. In fact, you won't find a linen white wall in any of the rooms in any of the homes I have owned. But this goes with my boisterous personality, and luckily, my not-so-boisterous husband loves it as well. I happen to like a lot of visual stimulation in my home. And for the record, my meditation room, the room I go to when I need to decompress, is painted a soft robin's egg blue. For me, life is too short to live with white walls, but I'm not so foolish as to believe that all my clients share that sentiment.

So in this situation, I was a little skeptical about recommending all this color in my client's newly-claimed interior. I had a nagging sense that her desire to break out of her formerly color-deprived imprisonment was more of a defensive reaction, rather than a thoughtfully considered choice that she could easily live with for the long-term. Well, she insisted on painting deep indigo blue on her dining room walls and rich eucalyptus green in her living room. By the time we got to her lemon yellow kitchen, it hit her that she had overeaten at the color buffet, so to speak. Alas, I had to instruct my painters to paint over all of the walls with white primer – we were back to the drawing board.

Enough psychology, you're thinking, right? What's the point? The point is learning to recognize the distinct "degrees" or levels of decorating that happen in every room. Think of Level Three as the accessories: the artwork, figurines, pillows, candles, etc. that are usually the last pieces to go into a room. Level Two consists of the furniture and window treatments, and Level One is the backdrop of every room: the walls, floors, and ceilings. Another way to describe this categorization is recognizing the Primary, Secondary, and Tertiary degrees of decorating a room. You may resemble my client who, in an attempt to express her liberated self, confused these levels. She thought she craved color and plenty of it and thus was going to bring in deep color at Level One of every room. Yet Level One is a particular commitment, whatever you choose to put there.

In this case, we did end up placing our color on Levels One and Two (or the Primary and Secondary degrees of decorating the room), but we toned down the intensity. For her dining room, we selected an Oriental area rug that had deep and medium blues, as well as clay, coral, and olive green tones. We did a faux painting treatment of soft clay on the walls and brought in a cadet blue (medium-toned) damask fabric on her dining room chairs. We found a lovely transitional fabric for the valance that had the same tones as the area rug. Finally, we found a charming painting for the main wall that also shared this color scheme.

In her living room, we chose another Oriental rug with medium tones of camel and cocoa, and for her two love seats we selected a gorgeous and colorful Old World tapestry. For the walls, we picked a color out of the tapestry fabric in a soft buttery toffee and did a faux treatment here as well. Pillows and other accessories picked up the other colors in the fabric, such as celadon, olive green, and burgundy. When we were through, all of the rooms boasted rich beautiful color, but in the proportion she could happily live with well into the future.

Scrumptious buttery toffee walls envelop the family room, perfect for rest and repose. Bolder colors of blue and brick are found in the Old World tapestry fabric we chose for the loveseats.

If you're still struggling with where and how much color to add to your interiors, I highly suggest visiting a bookstore, especially the ones that let you sip cappuccino while roaming the stacks. Select several books full of glossy pages of colored interiors, and imagine yourself living in those spaces. You can also visit one of the national home improvement stores that, in their paint department, offer a special computer station equipped with interior design programs. With the click of a button, these programs allow you to change the color of the walls and ceilings, and in some cases, the furnishings of the room, thereby allowing you to fully envision each specific effect. Finally, if you're agile on your own computer, you can purchase a myriad of interior design programs yourself and create a customized floor plan of your own home, including options for painted walls and furnishings.

In the end, it's up to you to decide if you love the vibrancy of a lot of color everywhere, or if you prefer the clean and calm feel of crisp white walls and colorful accessories. Whatever you decide – congratulations! You've just filled in another piece of your home décor puzzle and now you can venture forth in celebration of your authentic self.

A faux treatment of soft clay tones on the walls provided a beautiful backdrop for minimal furnishings in the intimate dining space.

Do You Want Your Home To Be Warm, Cool – Or Both?

Whether you're starting from scratch or just updating a room full of furniture you still like, it's important for you to choose a color palette with "temperature" in mind. While it's obvious that warm colors have yellow undertones and cool colors have blue undertones, for many clients, choosing a harmonious palette isn't always easy. The first step is to determine what a color's "temperature" is – warm or cool – then to decide which you like better. Traditionally, sticking to either a warm *or* a cool palette was considered by many people to be the only acceptable way to create a color palette. Now, however, as people are more willing to experiment with their interiors and are embracing color, thoughtful and careful combinations of warm and cool colors are very popular, and worth considering.

Determining if a color is warm or cool

The important thing to remember when choosing colors is that they are very relative, and almost like chameleons, express themselves differently in different situations. Invariably, when I bring six or seven swatches of, say, gold fabric to a client, the one that they thought looked yellow in the fabric store suddenly looks green next to their couch. Or a blue that had azure tones in it suddenly looks gray next to their teal pillow. Never make a decision in a vacuum; always compare colors to the other pieces that will be coexisting in the room.

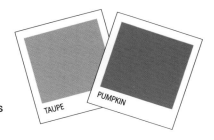

In this color combination, the warm and rich pumpkin tone is beautifully complimented with a warmer taupe, featuring cocoa hues.

And don't select colors in a showroom or retail store without having brought them home first to view them in the space. Showroom lighting is very different from the lighting that exists in most people's homes. Always bring home several fabric samples and see how they mingle in your existing space. When it comes to choosing paint, select at least three shades you're considering and paint test patches on the walls, in roughly 12x6-inch stripes. Paint on the darkest and lightest sections of your walls, and view them in the daylight as well as in artificial light in the evening. Ask yourself not only if you like each color, but also if it's too warm or too cool for the rest of the objects in the room. Once you've determined the temperature of your colors, you can then combine them with this characteristic in mind.

Warm and cool together

There are many popular combinations of warm and cool color palettes, such as blue and yellow, fuchsia and pumpkin, and the newest rage, blue and brown. While these combos look stunning together, you still need to be

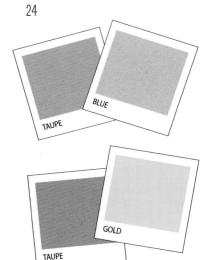

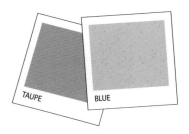

It's particularly popular today to mix warm and cool tones. While cool taupe looks modern and hip with blue, and the yellow undertones of a warm taupe look wonderful with a sunny yellow, notice the interesting tension created when you mix a cocoa-y warm taupe with icy blue. It's a wonderful marriage of opposites!

aware of the relative coolness or warmth of the hues you choose for a room, because *all* cool colors don't look good with *all* warm colors.

For example, there are countless variations of the color *taupe*; some have more brown undertones, some taupes are very gray. While the warmer versions of taupe can look wonderful with salmon, gold, and brick red, the cooler version of taupe with gray undertones may look harsh, and simply too cold, with these colors. Gray taupes look wonderful with similarly cool-toned colors such as periwinkle, plum, deep wine, and mint or celadon (gray) green. These color combinations tend to be more contemporary than traditional and lend themselves to an urban chic sensibility.

While cool shades of brown and taupe go well with soft pastel blue, the browns that look the most current and fresh when paired with icy blues are the warmer cocoa/milk chocolate browns. In this instance, it's a wonderful marriage of opposites.

So before you shake your heads in total confusion, the upshot is this: Some cool and warm tones look fabulous together, but that's not a general, across-the-board rule. It's probably safe to say that if you find yourself drawn to contrasts such as combining both warm and cool palettes in one room, you're probably drawn to contemporary rather than traditional style. You may like interiors with some inherent tension, an edge, if you will. And that's terrific, as long as you don't go overboard and end up with a room full of dissonance.

Warm and cool whites

Let me take a moment to talk about the toughest color to identify: white. White is the combination of all the colors of the visible spectrum of light, even though the human eye experiences it as an absence of color. There can be over thirty whites on a typical paint fan, making the statement "Let's just go with white" really confusing. Often, if a client is adamantly in favor of pure white, but I'm afraid it will look just too stark in their interior, I choose one of the many "tinted whites" readily available from most major paint manufacturers. When you see them lined up on their color brochure, it's obvious that none are *pure* white, but when viewed away from the contrast of the other thirty whites, the overall effect of a tinted white will still look fresh and neutral. Some are tinted with the slightest hint of green; others are slightly gray or brown. Yet on a wall, they will give you the best of both worlds: the simplicity and pureness of white, with just a suggestion of hue that rescues them from looking bland.

If you find yourself feeling most comfortable with white walls, yet you've decided on a warm palette, consider choosing a tinted white with just a dash of a warm tone, such as yellow or brown. Conversely, if you favor a cool palette, choose a tinted white with a smidgen of red (which will translate as the slightest rosy cast) or a touch of blue. Interestingly, even though green is *mostly* a warm color, when used in small concentrations with white it translates as a cool minty green, so keep this in mind if you have warm colors such as forest green, rust, and brown in your space. You're better off adding a drop of yellow or brown paint to your white base to keep an overall warm palette.

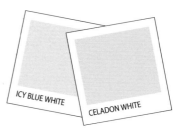

ICY BLUE WHITE

CELADON WHITE

So whether you're most comfortable in a purely warm or purely cool palette, or like to live on the edge with a contrasting palette in your space, have a ball! Experiment. Paint as many test strips on the wall as you need to until you're satisfied with just the right hue. Having an awareness of the relative warmth or coolness of colors will allow you make informed design decisions. You'll be amazed at the variety of colors you can combine in a room if you make your choices with this distinction in mind.

For some clients, even the paint chips on the very top of the paint fan are too much color. Not to worry; look for the paint manufacturer's fan of Tinted Whites. They add just a bit of hue to a white base, which usually rescues them from looking stark or shocking.

This elegant living room just exudes sophistication thanks to the cohesive palette of buttery yellow walls, warm red textiles, and deep rich wood tones. Note that the dark mahogany furniture not only adds formality to the space but stands up to the intense color concentration; lighter-toned woods would have easily been overshadowed by such robust color.

What's Your Tolerance For Mixing Prints And Patterns?

This is a very personal decision. As a designer, I always try to offer the most attractive and striking combination of patterns while absolutely respecting a client's personal limits. Many novices play it safe by having one pattern and all solids in a given room. I urge you to experiment with mixing plaids and florals, or paisleys and stripes. Many fabric companies have made this process easier for you by creating what they call **companion fabrics**, i.e., two, three, and four patterns all designed to exist harmoniously in one room. This way, all you have to do is choose a color palette you like, and the patterns are already coordinated for you.

An example of a set of coordinates might be: a large floral, a smaller floral, a stripe, and a check, all of which are made from the *exact* same set of dyes in the *same* hue. This is why they work. We're not mixing pastels with primary colors, or muted and vibrant jewel tones. Coordinated fabrics are all variations on the same color scheme; they are just translated in several complimentary patterns that elevate a room from nice to fabulous when paired together.

If you find a fabric you love and it doesn't come with its own coordinate fabrics, fear not. Of course you can create your own ensembles by selecting your own coordinate fabrics, but admittedly, this takes a little practice. Be aware that there's more to a fabric than simply its color. All fabrics have a personality, or a *feel*, as we say in the trade. Most people would identify damask, for example, as a formal fabric, even if they didn't know its rightful name! Conversely, most people would agree that muslin or gingham plaid are examples of casual, informal fabrics. These levels of formality absolutely come into play when you're choosing coordinates for a design project.

Loud and boisterous colors and patterns typify the personality of these clients! Note that animal prints act almost as neutrals when paired with the splash of intense colors found in the contemporary pennant valance and ottoman.

For example, a client of mine did a nice job of finding what she considered to be coordinate fabrics to go with a main fabric we found for her master bedroom duvet cover. While the fabrics she chose matched exactly in hue, unfortunately they were the wrong texture. We were planning to make her duvet in a poly silk blend, but the coordinates she selected were all woven. The woven fabrics looked too casual sitting next to the shiny and elegant poly silk. When I suggested we stay with the formality of the poly silk blend by selecting coordinates such as damasks or silk jacquards, both of which have a slight sheen, she thought for a moment. She decided she found herself liking the warm informality of the woven fabrics better than the poly silk she had originally chosen for the duvet!

This story illustrates two important points about managing a design project: (1) My client learned something about choosing complimentary fabrics: you should look not only at the color and hue of fabrics but also the personality the fabric is conveying. And (2) it really helps to be flexible when working on a design project. Rather than feeling like she was stuck moving in a particular direction, my client listened to her heart, and in fact, decided she preferred to abandon her original plan of a formal master bedroom, replete with shiny fabrics and regal patterns. Instead, she began to visualize a country cozy ambiance full of woven florals and coordinating paper silks. We stuck with her original plan to fill the room with rich berry and plum tones but now the overall effect was less stuffy. We added a bunch of throw pillows, some custom-made of varying shades of paper silk, while other needlepoint pillows were purchased at a local boutique. The final accent to the room was adding a re-upholstered lady's chair in a yellow and berry woven floral, with a plum chenille throw. Positively yummy!

Finally, if the thought of multiple patterns in a room gives you the willies, at least offset the solid fabrics with the use of texture (see Custom Treatments, page 93). Tone-on-tones, jacquards, and moirés will offer great interest by virtue of their innate textural appeal, yet they are still considered solid, not patterned.

This lovely valance and matching pillows were store-bought. Increasingly, companies are making coordinated separates such as valances, pillows, table runners, and placemats that have a decidedly custom look for a fraction of the price.

Chapter Three
Basic Considerations

Couldn't We All Use A Little More Balance?

I recently started working with a lovely couple. While in their family room, the husband said, "I really need symmetry – I can't stand that there are bookshelves on one side of the television and a built-in nook on the other side." I really hate to stereotype, but I calmly asked him, "Are you an engineer?" He replied "yes" and luckily all three of us laughed. He wasn't offended; rather, he proudly embraced his need for order and symmetry.

Balance is achieved in this beach-side guest room with a retro feel. Unmatched side tables and lamps are a perfect fit for a casual room that looks airy and not overly contrived.

What about you? Do you find yourself favoring symmetry over balance... Or even wondering what the difference is? The classic place where this issue arises is in the decoration of a fireplace mantel. *Symmetry* means that if you visually cut the mantel in half, both sides would be a mirror image of each other. A typical scenario would be a large mirror in the center of the mantel and a candlestick lamp on either corner. *Balance*, on the other hand, means

objects aren't identical on both sides of the mantel, but they are balanced in scale and, ideally, mood. Picture this same fireplace with a mirror in the center, but this time one side has a pair of chunky and ornate candlesticks, and the other side displays the bust of Julius Caesar, for example. Both the symmetrical and balanced mantels are attractive, but the latter is a bit less conservative; less "matchy-matchy," as the expression goes.

The same rule applies when decorating sofa tables, buffets, sideboards, and hall consoles. In the photo of the sideboard to the right, you'll see how we achieved a balanced look without necessarily using symmetry. The three topiaries nicely balanced the three-tiered plate rack because all of the objects were of similar scale.

Think about balance when you contemplate decorating your bedrooms. I once had a client who wouldn't even entertain the thought of non-matching nightstands in his master bedroom, even when the pieces I suggested were all from the same furniture line! "That's what my parents always had; that's what I want," he insisted. This is certainly a personal decision, but I can tell you that your interiors will look far more interesting if you give yourself permission to shoot for balance and not

In this garden-inspired dining room, notice the flea market bureau that was reincarnated as a buffet. Varied but balanced accessories make for an eye-catching tablescape.

necessarily symmetry. Picture a British Colonial-styled bedroom with one night table made of chunky dark stained wicker, and a small bamboo chest for the other. Add two mahogany Victorian unmatched bureaus and the look is positively smashing, and nothing matches! Especially if you unite the furniture with coordinating bedding, window treatments, and appropriate accessories, the effect is striking and just a bit more fashion-forward than symmetrical arrangements. I apologize if I offended any engineers out there…

Embrace Feng Shui, Even If Just A Little

For those of you who have no knowledge of Feng Shui, let me give you a quick explanation. Feng Shui (pronounced "Fung-Shway") is the ancient Chinese art of placement, which maintains that the objects in our environment directly impact all aspects of our lives, including our health, prosperity, and relationships.

The art has been around for over 5,000 years in Eastern cultures, and for the last fifteen years or so has gained increased popularity in Western culture. Unfortunately, our culture is skeptical and slow to catch on to progressive ideas such as Feng Shui, but I can tell you that no building is erected in the Far East without a Feng Shui analysis. Architects and surveyors carefully advise builders about the optimal placement of not only the structure in relation to the land, but the positions of the doors and windows and wall placement within the building. But Feng Shui isn't limited to major construction projects; it applies to all aspects of your home, from the structural layout of the rooms to the placement of the smallest of decorative accessories.

Feng Shui is also as much about symbolism and metaphors as it is about placement of furniture. For example, I often try to persuade clients to avoid hanging ceiling fans over their beds. Many swear by them and refuse to give them up. Is it likely that the fan will spin wildly out of control and decapitate them whilst they sleep? Probably not. But because of the symbolism of the whirling blades, fans are foreboding and present an ominous energy, and this is why bedroom fans aren't great Feng Shui. Another example of poor Feng Shui is having your back to the door of your home or work office. Is it likely that a coworker will sneak up from behind and stab you to death and rob you of your trade secrets? Most likely not. But again, anyone who is even remotely intuitive will say they don't feel terribly comfortable with their backs to the door of their office. If you can't rearrange your office so that you face your door, the easiest fix is to hang a large mirror on an adjacent wall so that you can see someone entering the office in the reflection. Feng Shui is essentially about using common sense in a nontraditional way to make your spaces as comfortable, functional, and balanced as possible.

As a designer, I have come to learn two truths about Feng Shui: (1) Feng Shui is powerful, transformative, and available to all. While there are now hundreds of books on the subject, one of my favorites is *Home Design with Feng Shui A-Z* by Terah Kathryn Collins. It's a primer, a quick reference guide that makes Feng Shui accessible and easy to follow. It's also an absolute feast for the eyes, filled with lush and colorful illustrations. I've also learned that (2) most interior designers do *not* decorate with Feng Shui in mind. A room may be visually lovely, but still quite out of balance on Feng Shui terms. For example, a room that's richly painted and appointed entirely in gold and red is considered to be excessive in fire energy, which can cause a volatile, argumentative atmosphere. Too little fire energy, on the other hand, can cause fear of the future and fatigue. It's all about balance!

The good news is that you don't have to become an expert on Feng Shui to have a more beautiful and balanced interior. Even a little awareness of Feng Shui is better than none at all. Just a few small improvements to your interiors made with Feng Shui in mind will have the power to transform. Since you picked up this book, I'm guessing you're looking for fresh ideas. What better time than now to begin anew, to take stock of what works and make plans to "raise the bar" in any aspect of our lives? Home is where the heart is, so why not begin right there?

Here are some very easy Feng Shui corrections you can do in your home today; I invite you to try them and see if you feel any difference:

1. Hang a mirror over your stovetop. (Yes it will get splattered from time to time, but do it!) For the same reasons why your back ideally shouldn't be facing your home or office door, the mirror over the stove reflects the view behind you. I have to admit when I first read about this suggestion, I thought I would hate the way it looked. But I couldn't believe the visceral feeling of comfort I felt when I hung my first mirror over my stove.

2. Dispose of all dead or faded and crispy dried flower arrangements and replace with silk flowers or real ones if time and money allow. Dead anything around the house isn't great Feng Shui.

3. Keep the drains of your tub and sinks closed when not in use, and always close your toilet seat. In Feng Shui, vital energy, also called Ch'i is just like water; it can be pulled down the drain or flushed down the toilet very easily.

4. Remove any artwork whose subject matter is violent or unpleasant. Need I say more? (Although fans of Picasso's *Geurnica* would probably eschew this belief.)

The Chinese have identified areas of a space in which particular activities thrive, using the traditions of I Ching. Place this template – called a Bagua chart – over a floorplan of your home to see which activities are encouraged in which rooms. Because your home is a physical expression of your life, the Bagua will help you identify which areas are suffering and how to improve them.

5. Peruse your home and remove any objects that have an inauspicious past (i.e., remnants of a past relationship that ended badly). Feng Shui believes that all objects carry energy, and in these cases, the energy is negative. Don't you want to be surrounded by the most positive energy possible? Even if you don't believe that inanimate objects carry energy, have you ever looked at your ex-wife's/husband's end table and felt annoyed or angry? Why live with that?

6. Paint your front entrance door a shade of red, or a least place some red objects near your front door, such as red flowers or a red doormat. In Feng Shui, red, being the color of passion, is thought to attract prosperity, celebration, and joy into the home if placed in or near its entrance.

7. Consider asking guests to remove their shoes upon entering your home. Provide them a basket or rack to store their shoes and offer them socks or booties to wear while they are visiting. This means *you* need to remove your shoes as well (particularly challenging for some husbands…). A shoeless home symbolizes leaving your worldly cares and concerns at the door.

An art that has survived the test of time for 5,000 years is certainly worth considering, especially if you suffer from unsatisfying relationships, stalled wealth accumulation, or perhaps troubled physical health. If there are parts of your life that you think can use some improvement or are in need of a renaissance, so to speak, you would be wise to look into the transformative powers of Feng Shui. As I stated earlier, a little Feng Shui is good, a lot is better.

In Feng Shui, the color of red is thought to attract prosperity, celebration, and joy into the home. It's particularly important that this color be used at your home's entrance, the place of first impressions. This home is doubly blessed because not only did the occupants paint their front door red, but they adorned their entrance with beautiful red flowers.

Follow Your Nose To An Inviting Atmosphere

Have you ever entered someone's home and, while it was visually lovely, you just couldn't get by the fact that it smelled like wet schnauzer? Or perhaps you were bowled over by the smell of mothballs upon entering? Sadly, I've met both of these interiors firsthand… No, not in my house, but yes, in clients' homes! Since I'm an avid enthusiast of feeding all of the senses, especially our noses, I urge you to consider using scent as a way to further define your home's personality.

I was once hired by a client to get her house ready for sale. She liked the idea of simmering cinnamon sticks and orange peels in a pot of water on the stove whenever her realtor held an open house. This was especially appropriate because she lived in the woods in an authentic country setting.

Houseplants are another wonderful and natural way to add scent to the air. Especially in early spring, forcing bulbs such as Narcissus and Hyacinths will add a sweet and pungent aroma to your space. Potted herbs such as rosemary, mint, basil, and tarragon will work double duty to scent your kitchen and flavor your culinary creations.

If you tend to favor a lower-maintenance method of scenting your home, pleasant aromas can be found in a myriad of forms, including candles, sprays, potpourri, and "plug-in" oils and gel packs. And none of these forms require frequent watering! Of course, with all candles, use precaution. Never leave a lit candle unattended, and if you tend to purchase bargain candlesticks, watch how they burn. I personally witnessed a bargain taper candle unexpectedly burn so rapidly and so unevenly that the flame was three inches high when we hastily covered it with a saucepan to extinguish it!

Notwithstanding that little horror story, candles not only add lovely scent to your space but

Whether you choose pillars or tapers, float them in water, or nestle them in a bed of tumbled stones, candles infuse your space with instant ambiance, tranquility, and often delightful fragrance.

incredible ambiance. What is the easiest way to add glamour to your home? Candles – as many as you can stand. Almost any clear vessel will do as a container for candles; just make sure you allow enough room on the sides so the flames don't touch the glass. Good examples are brandy glasses, vintage sherbet cups, and for a more contemporary look, tall straight drinking glasses, frosted or clear, tinted or white. Ideally, use votive candles with metal cups to avoid any melted wax mess and group the candles in odd numbers (three or five is best) with varying heights for a striking display. If you're worried about melted wax sticking to your containers, just put a bit of water in the bottom of the vessel; the wax will ball up in the water instead of sticking to the glass. And on this subject, do yourself a favor and purchase a tin of sticky wax, designed to help keep candles, especially tapers, in place and upright. It's made from – you guessed it – wax, and some type of putty adhesive. You put a small blob of it on the bottom of your tapers and they will sit tight in their holders.

When scenting your space, consider matching the scents to your home's décor. As I mentioned above, my client who lived in a country cottage setting loved the homespun scents of cinnamon and nutmeg. If you, on the other hand, live in a chic urban loft with clean lines, you might be drawn to sophisticated scents such as sandalwood, sage, or "crisp cotton."

If matching scents to your décor feels too limiting, definitely consider changing the scents with the seasons. In cooler months, scents such as cinnamon, pumpkin, holly berry, and pine are wonderful. As the weather warms up, we intuitively want to start smelling light floral scents such as lilac and daylily, or fabulous fruity aromas such as pear and tangerine.

If you're looking for a source for great candles, I'd like to recommend the company of a woman I met at a local crafts fair in Duxbury, MA awhile back. It's called Candles by K, and Karen produces lovely, unique, and positively scrumptious-smelling candles and gift sets. Like me, Karen turned her passion into a career; I'm always happy to patronize small or home-based local businesses. I hope you'll consider some of her lovely products. Mention my name!

New on the market are the small bottles of scented oil with thin bamboo sticks or reeds sitting in the oil to disperse the scent in the air through absorption. These are fabulous choices if you don't want to deal with the dicey issue of lit candles, especially if you have pets or small children running around the house.

When you take advantage of the many options for scenting your home that not only add wonderful atmosphere but look great while doing it, you'll begin to feel that you've discovered an entirely new way to enjoy and experience your space. Here's to new discoveries!

Couples Need To Learn To Compromise

In my experience, it's the exception and not the rule that couples have the same taste in interior design. Interestingly, even the gay couples with whom I've worked seem to have distinctly different tastes, so it may not be gender-related. Because in love opposites often attract, it's to be expected that these "opposite" couples will also process information differently. They probably have distinct natures and different temperaments; it stands to reason that they will be attracted to different colors, textures, and décors.

I have an amusing memory from a few years ago, when I was working with a professional couple. He was an engineer, and she was an attorney with a very creative, artistic nature. She asked me to bring some contemporary abstract artwork for their approval. He gazed at the prints and, with an expression bordering on repulsion, muttered, "Why do you like these?" She immediately became defensive and blurted out several intellectual reasons why modern art is important and how these pieces reflected the inner turmoil of the artist etc., etc. I delicately suggested that unknowingly, Hubby asked a trick question, that is to say one that had neither a right nor wrong answer. The bottom line is we love what we love because we love it.

Even we interior designers have to do a good job of selling our honeys on our wild and crazy décor ideas. In my home, wh all else fails, "trust me" is my promise.

I counsel my couples clients not to ask their honeys to explain. Taste is highly personal and often idiosyncratic. Instead, try to find a common ground.

One exercise I highly recommend is to go to the interior design section of one of the large national bookstores in your area, you know, the ones that play great music and have comfy plush easy chairs for you to sit and read in. Select four or five books that depict particular design styles, such as craftsman, country, retro, Zen, traditional, etc. In a non-judgmental tone, simply flip through the books together and tell each other which styles appeal to you most.

Then, to make this exercise really count, I ask each person to make three columns on a sheet of paper. One column lists your absolute favorites, the middle column lists your "I can live with this" choices, and the last column lists the styles you absolutely can't tolerate. For a ready-made chart, photocopy the Couples chart in the Appendix and take it to the bookstore with you.

I can assure you that this exercise really does work; the visual aids provided by the photos and the act of writing down one's preferences really articulates each person's point of view and encourages couples to find a common ground.

For example, I had a female client who loved country style. Her husband hated it. This exercise revealed that in actuality it was her love of hens and roosters and faded gingham fabric that her husband couldn't tolerate. Then the husband went through the books and selected Shaker style furniture. While the wife would have initially selected chunky Early American furniture, she also found herself drawn to the Shaker style her husband loved. Lo and behold, they realized they suddenly had a joint style. His clean-lined Shaker pieces would blend seamlessly with her country sensibility. She gave up her washed-out gingham fabrics in favor of bright and cheerful French provincial fabrics. Her hens and roosters were replaced with antique coffee pots, clocks, watering cans, and other rough-hewn objects from a simpler time. The couple was thrilled that their home was taking on a new personality, and they were heartened to see that they shared more commonalities than they previously believed. Cupid strikes again!

This sweet little den is a good example of couples compromising: He got the informal nonchalance he wanted from the wicker rocker and futon. She got the elegance and coziness she needed from the coordinated designer fabrics and perky swags.

Part II:
Wit and Wisdom

So by now, you're hopefully inspired. You've decluttered your space so all that's left is what you absolutely need and want to surround yourself with. Yet you may have a room that's mostly complete, but something about it feels awkward and you can't put your finger on why that is. Or you may have just moved into a home where the ceilings are very high and you'd like to do something about the cavernous feeling of the rooms. Here is where I discuss a lot of the common areas clients tend to get stuck, or stalled, in their design process.

I discuss what I (hesitate to) call the design rules: the nitty-gritty principles that will make your design process easier. I touch upon each of the design elements in your home you may be considering upgrading, such as buying and arranging your furniture; optimizing area rugs; and hanging, grouping, and framing artwork. I also spend a good amount of time on those pesky but glorious topics that come up time and again with my clients: making sense of color and fabric. I happily offer up some tricks of the trade on creating illusions and minimizing unattractive elements in your rooms. Finally, I've provided specific ideas on how to transform the individual rooms in your home, such as your master bedroom, kitchen, bathroom, and home office. The spiritual therapist in me couldn't finish this section without strongly encouraging you to create a special spot, a sacred space of your very own in your home, however small it may be. Again, most of these ideas were inspired by rooms I've been in over the years that presented a particular design challenge for my clients. We conquered the challenge for them and I hope I can help conquer the challenge for you too. Enjoy! Take notes if you like. ☺

Chapter Four
Decorating Process

Makeovers Need Not Be Expensive Or Extreme

While "extreme everything" is de rigueur these days, I think the average person gets extremely inert when it comes to tackling overwhelming challenges, and decorating can be just that, so let's start small!

I was recently hired by a couple who really didn't like the house they'd been living in for the past three years. I think they thought its idiosyncrasies

Can you say hand-me-down Rose? The Mediterranean chairs were from the in-laws, the mirror over the fireplace was from Goodwill, and the area rug cost all of $100. Yet this eclectic salon boasts drama and original style, with warmth and coziness, all with a very modest budget.

would grow on them, but they hadn't. So much of their pleasure seemed to lie in the future, if only they could "gut this" and "rip that out." Yet these big renovations would not be feasible for another two to three years. They had been totally immobilized by the daunting prospect of redecorating; not knowing where on Earth to begin, yet knowing they couldn't afford to do all that they wanted to. I was brought in to ignore these "un-usable rooms" and help them with a few other rooms. I gently challenged them with the following thought: What if I could make these "un-usable rooms" lovely and habitable so they didn't hate and resent them? Then in two to three years, when their budget allowed, they could begin the big renovations, and design the rooms of their dreams. The couple nodded in unison, as if a warm wave of relief had just washed over their bodies.

This couple realized that for just about $5,000, including all of the labor costs to paint the ceiling, walls, and wainscoting, they could get a stunning finished formal dining room. So here was the plan:

• They chose a red, gold, and black Oriental area rug that nicely anchored the space. They saved some money here by buying a machine-made, rather than handmade, wool rug.

• We shopped together at a local discount outlet for new furniture. After debating the ubiquitous issue of contemporary vs. traditional, they opted for a clean-lined, dark-stained (sometimes called espresso) contemporary table and matching hutch. They paid $100 for the table because it had a few little nicks on it, which we covered with furniture markers.

• We added six parsons chairs upholstered in a gorgeous Old World gold and red brocade fabric; the chairs were only $85 each.

• We painted a dramatic russet red color on the walls, linen white on the ceiling, and creamy golden caramel on the wainscoting. The paint job was the most expensive piece of the project, and when you're on a budget, this is an area where you shouldn't skimp. The paint job will either make or destroy the integrity of the room's design, so all in all, my clients spent very wisely.

• A contemporary brushed nickel chandelier was a crisp nod to the clean-lined furnishings and kept the room from looking too traditional. They also saved quite a bit of money by using their own artwork and final accessories.

Originally, this couple was perfectly willing to ignore one-seventh of their home until they were financially able to handle the major renovation they planned to do three years into the future. That would have squandered one-seventh of their mortgage payment, not to mention the psychological downer of looking into an empty, unfinished dining room every time they sat in the family room or kitchen. So instead of spending $25,000 for an extreme renovation, they spent $5,000 and are as happy as clams. If in a few years they end up taking out the back wall of the dining room to add six more feet, terrific. But in the meantime, they have a fetching dining room where they are proud to entertain family and friends, just as it exists today.

I think it takes patience and creativity to figure out the least stressful/expensive/disruptive way to make over a room. And when you're viscerally distressed in a room badly in need of new décor, it's hard to be either patient or creative. My best advice: make a list of all the things you'd like to improve upon and decide what would be both the high- and low-impact versions of making improvements (impact is defined by cost outlay, disruption of your family life, and potential stress level). For example, in a kitchen or bathroom where you have unsightly tiles, the high-impact

This sweet country dining room got a major facelift by simply lightening up its heavy, dated look. The owners removed the dark green wallpaper, painted the walls a fresh and soft pastel hue, then had a decorative artist add a floral stencil above the chair rail. Editing out some of the china plates and trinkets also created a new airy look. For a few hundred dollars and some elbow grease, the dining room was reborn.

way of improving would be to remove the tiles. The low-impact way could be painting over the tiles with one of the new high-tech tile adhesive paints.

Ask your friends and neighbors where you can find local off-price retail stores. They are plentiful these days. Read the paper, especially the Sunday circulars, for sales and promotions being offered. You can find bedding and linens, simple window treatments, endless accessories, and even low-cost area rugs at many national discount stores – almost anything you'd ever need for a low-impact makeover.

With decorating made this easy, you can leave the extreme behavior to the teenagers, while you practice some extreme relaxation in your new interiors.

Big Money Doesn't Equate To Big Taste

Aren't you glad to read this? It's absolutely true. Spending a lot of money on furnishings and home accessories may mean they're valuable or well-built, but it doesn't guarantee that you'll have a cohesive and attractive end result. There has never been a time in recent history when so much variety of styles and price points existed in the home furnishings field as it does today, so now, more than ever, you don't need to spend a fortune to decorate your home beautifully. I often advise clients to spend a bigger chunk of their budget on something very meaningful to them, such as a handmade wool rug, or an exquisitely carved armoire. These pieces will instantly elevate the look of the room, thereby allowing more affordable accessories to coexist.

In this vein, one of my favorite installations was the Monet-inspired dining room I did for a client about ten years ago. She loved the *Waterlilies* series of prints by Monet, and she wanted to highlight the soft minty celadon green tones, more than the lilac purple tones, in her room. So we sponged her walls with three shades of green and accented with some lilac tinted glaze. (We also painted her favorite affirmations along the ceiling line.) Since it was a small room, we kept the furnishings to a minimum. We ordered the pedestals for the table from a catalog, but we had the glass tabletop cut by a local glass-cutter (about twenty-five percent less expensive than through the catalog). The four parsons chairs were only $90 each, purchased at a local retailer. (Note: Make sure your room doesn't look too airy when using a large glass tabletop; medium-toned paint on the walls provided a lot of definition for this room. The room would have visually "floated away" had we kept the walls white.)

The real gem in the room was a mid-century bureau we found, no joke, by the side of the road. We sponged on a base coat of soft lilac then had my decorative painter stencil on some rosebud vines. We spray-painted the nicked and pitted handles, which made them look like new. This bureau was reincarnated as a buffet that offered tons of storage for linens, dishes, candles, etc.

While this dining room was small, it was flooded with natural light, thanks to the wall of windows opposite the buffet wall. To maximize the light, we purposely did not add fabric window treatments. Instead, in keeping with the garden theme my client loved, we strung natural grape vine coils across the tops of the window casings and filled the vines with ivy and silk hydrangeas. The final bargain was the iron chandelier we picked at a local home supplies warehouse for $140! My client had breakfast each morning bathed in sunlight, and when she entertained dinner guests, she felt like they were dining in Monet's garden.

In this delightful sun-drenched space, the mid-century bedroom bureau reincarnated as a buffet was an endless conversation piece. However, the elegant chandelier picked up at a home improvement superstore provided some competition for the cleverest use of minimal cash.

Remember that haute and humble items can happily coexist in any room of your house. And another benefit of *not* paying top dollar on all items is that you're free to guiltlessly change your mind every couple of years and replace pieces, without having to refinance the house. Your financial planner (and maybe your spouse) will be glad you bought this book.

You Can Have It All: Order and Aesthetics

In the last ten to fifteen years, organizing has been elevated to a new art form. As I mentioned on page 16, there are literally hundreds of good books on organizing and, more important, hundreds of readily available retail sources of great organizing tools and systems. It has never been easier or more affordable to purchase chests of drawers, cubbies, containers, racks, and shelving in all kinds of materials and styles. In other words, there simply is no longer any excuse for being disorganized! The best part of all of this is that the newly-organized home is meant to be displayed, not relegated to the shelves in your closet.

This 1800s Mansard Colonial home boasted many lovely features, including these built-in bookcases in the living room. Candles are stored in the leather chest on one shelf, while photo boxes below hold hundreds of captured family moments. Why not be functional and attractive at the same time?

For clients who don't have a lot of closet space, I tell them not to worry. If they have a blank wall and some decent ceiling height, the solution is as simple as a bookcase. There are a myriad of storage containers that are very attractive and obviously functional that look great tucked into a bookcase. For home offices, wicker bins, hat boxes, cardboard photo boxes, and some of the new vinyl lidded boxes are just a few examples of storage containers that can neatly hold pads of papers and file folders, not to mention small office supplies such as staples, pens, pencils, and paperclips. I keep the mini tape measures I give to my clients on a bookshelf in a beautiful Italian ceramic biscotti canister. If you need additional storage in your bedroom, these containers can easily accommodate scarves, belts, socks, and hosiery, as well as non-bulky clothing such as T-shirts and workout attire.

When you're using your shelving to store books, try to resist filling every square inch with just books. I know most academicians would scoff with contempt at such a suggestion, but visually, our eyes need relief. Bookshelves look far more striking and inviting when we balance our books with photos, statuettes, candles, and any other objets d'art that appeal to you. Try to fill only about half of the bookshelf with books stacked either horizontally or vertically, then disperse other items around the books in the open spaces, as we did in the photo to the left. Try to avoid filling one shelf entirely with one type of object, such as books, the other shelf entirely with CDs, and the next shelf entirely with photos, for example. It's the mix that makes it special.

I once had a client who had a lovely collection of blown glass ornaments and paperweights that she wanted to display on her oak bookshelves. She loved the look of lit bookshelves but didn't like the contemporary look of glass shelving, which is often necessary if you want the light to shine down through the entire bookcase. Solution: we had a carpenter rout out the centers of each shelf and drop in a pane of glass. Then we hung small cabinet lights inside the top shelf. Thanks to the glass inserts, the light washed all the way down through the many shelves of the bookcase, and the oak edge of the shelves gave the traditional and substantial look she hoped for.

I could write for chapters on beautiful organization that looks as good as it functions, but there are many good books that have already done that, so just let me leave you with a quick list of some of my favorite objects that you can procure immediately to give your interiors an instant organizational face-lift:

In this bedroom turned home office, the closet was reconfigured to meet the storage needs of a busy business. Wicker bins and cubbies are the next best thing to sliced low-carb bread, especially when your storage shelves are constantly in public view, as are these, since the closet doors were removed for easier accessibility.

1. Pot racks
2. Wine racks
3. Zippered binders for CDs (for those who haven't moved on to MP3 players); they allow you to dispose of bulky plastic CD cases and file the binders in your beautiful bookcases!
4. Hang-able shoe bags with plastic pouches to hold large jewelry pieces
5. Tension pole shower caddy

Remember, you'll enjoy your newly decorated interior far better when your clutter is under control and you can put you finger on something at a moment's notice.

Chapter Five
Furniture and Arrangements

Don't Judge A Couch By Its Fabric

Or loveseat, or side chair, or any other store-bought upholstered item. At least initially, try to overlook the pattern and color of the fabrics found on the floor models. What is truly essential is that you like its lines, scale, and dimensions, and most important, that the piece of furniture is comfortable – these are qualities you can't change about your couch once you buy it. And chances are, once you've chosen the couch form, you'll have many choices for the fabric, so the color of the floor model shouldn't influence your purchasing decision.

Comfort

Sit on every piece you're considering, and try to imagine yourself relaxing at home. Does your back feel supported – or do you feel like you're doing abdominal crunches? Are your feet dangling off the edge? Is it too firm, or on the contrary, do you fear being swallowed in its puffy cushions, never to be seen alive again? You get the idea. Comfort first, then lines, size, and scale.

Lines

The lines of a couch are the first expressions of its style; a couch with straight edges and angular corners will look much more modern than one with rounded edges and arms. Couches with rounded detailing can either look casual, with big fluffy rolled arms, or traditional, with the tight detailing of a Queen Ann style. Also make sure you pay attention to the legs: chunky wooden legs or round feet, called **bun feet**, tend to look colonial or casual country. Ornately carved legs, a.k.a. **cabriole legs**, are typical of the traditional Queen Anne style, as are legs hidden by a kick-skirt. Finally, a solid wooden platform looks very mid-century modern, as do straight tapered legs, which have an Asian or Zen feel about them.

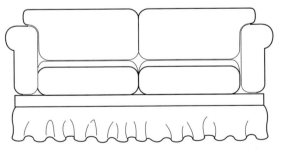
Country couch

Size

Once you like the way the couch looks and feels, don't forget to make sure it will work in your room! Measure carefully to make sure that it will not only fit in the space you intend to put it, but that it will also fit through any openings in your house it will need to go through to get to that space. On that note, make sure you've measured any doorways and other openings before you go to the store, so you know how much room you have. There's nothing worse than buying a beautiful couch that you love and finding out that it won't fit through your front door!

Scale

Now that you know the couch will be able to get into your room, pay attention to its scale in relation to the room. Rooms with low ceilings and little natural light might be better with more modern, low-slung pieces of furniture that don't overwhelm the space. Rooms with higher ceilings that are open to other spaces might need a heavier-looking piece of furniture to visually fill up the space and anchor your seating area. Think about how the couch will fit in with the overall feel of the room; with the seemingly endless options for couch styles, you'll be sure to find one that works in your space.

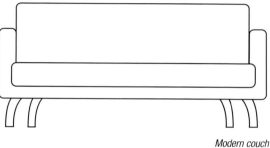

Modern couch

Fabric

Now that you have the "bones" chosen, fabric will come into play. Need help selecting a fabric? Your first decisions will be between fabric and leather; if you choose fabric, will it be solid or patterned? Most retail showrooms offer a myriad of fabric choices to go with their furniture lines. You don't need to gain access to the expensive designer showrooms in your town necessarily, just the attractive retail stores that have sufficient floor space. They tend to do a very nice job of putting together complete furniture sets, showing how different fabrics coexist in a room.

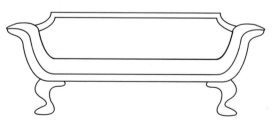

Vintage couch

I once worked with a client who wanted, in no uncertain terms, three different patterns in her family room: one for the sofa, another for the loveseat, and yet another for the side chair. She said she interviewed two other designers who refused to work with her because of this requirement. I smiled and told her it would be a little busy, but based on the scale of the room, the high ceiling, and terrific light – sure, we could do that.

When purchasing a piece of store-bought furniture, try to picture it wearing a white sheet. While in a showroom, you may be passing by many a lovely sofa because you are turned off by the fabric.

We ended up with a large yellow, pink, and blue floral for the sofa, a blue cabana stripe for the side chair, and a pink plaid for the loveseat, all in the same tones. We did the room in a garden theme with silk hydrangeas, wicker baskets, and garden figurines throughout. Yes, it was busy, but it frankly looked like a lush wildflower garden, with a multitude of colors in bloom. It all comes down to your preferences; just make sure you've selected the furniture first based on comfort and style, second on size and scale, and finally on color/fabric.

A final word on selecting furnishings: if among the many fabric choices a retail store offers, you don't see one you really like, ask the sale person if they will let you bring in your own fabric, otherwise known as COM (customer's own material). Not all retail stores will allow this, and know that this is a more expensive option because you're paying for the sofa *and* the 8-12 yards of fabric it takes to cover it, but it can be worth it if it means you're truly happy with your furniture.

Avoid Creating "Dance Floors" In Your Rooms

Very frequently, especially when I'm in the living and family rooms of my clients, I see furnishings pressed up against their walls, leaving large spaces in the center of the room. I call this the "dance floor" look – you know, pick

your partner and swing her round and round! For starters, this isn't the most attractive placement of furniture. It is, however, most conducive to eyestrain if you're watching TV, as well as yelling across the room to your guests when you're trying to entertain.

I'm not sure why people put all their furnishings against the walls; it certainly makes sense in a small room so there is adequate space to walk around. But in larger rooms, it's as if people need permission to pull away from the walls and fill the inner "void" of the space.

A large decorative screen and lush tropical plant beautifully fill the awkward space at the end of this living room. The zebra rug anchors the space while furniture and decorative objects float around it.

Filling in your space

So go ahead, experiment by pulling your furnishings into the center of the room, creating intimate conversation areas. If you're concerned that there's too much dead space behind the furnishings, add a sofa table behind the sofa or loveseat, or against the wall between two windows. On the sofa table, add a small table lamp, a small plant, candles, and/or picture frames, depending on the length of the table and the availability of a discrete electrical outlet. (Don't place a lamp on any surface unless the cord is safely tucked away under a piece of furniture – you don't want to create a tripping hazard!) Additional floor space can be filled with a variety of accessories, such as trees (real or faux), bamboo hampers and chests, vintage leather suitcases stacked on top of each other, and figurines/statues that are least three feet high, just to name a few. Another unusual accessory you can use to fill open spaces is a decorative screen. The most popular screens seen these days are made of wicker and rattan, but they are available in a myriad of styles. Three- and four-panel screens are available in painted finishes featuring traditional designs such as botanicals, or for the wild at heart, get a screen covered in a lacquered leopard print. For the family who loves to display photos, paneled screens are available with built-in 8x10-inch picture frames, usually holding fifteen to twenty images.

Angling your furniture

You can also consider angling the furniture to take up more space, which I describe more fully on page 56. In a living room or family room, angle your biggest piece of furniture, which is usually the sofa, across from something interesting, be it a fireplace or a view of the outside. Place your side chairs across from the sofa and ideally place a functional surface in between, such as a coffee table or an oversized fabric or leather ottoman. If you have an area rug, usually this is also angled along the same plane as the sofa.

Conversation areas

If you're lucky enough to have one of those living rooms that's twenty feet long or longer, then you have the option of setting up two or three distinct conversation areas. In the living room of one of my long-standing clients' home, we have their grand piano at one end of the room; the main sofa, coffee table, and two wing chairs in the center of the room in front of the fireplace; and at the far end, we placed a lovely antique chaise lounge, otherwise known as a fainting couch, with a lamp and small table for her tea cup. The worst thing to do in this type of living room is treat it as one long room. Trust me, when you entertain, you'll either have to use megaphones or drag your chairs all over the room to get close to your guests.

Notice how an intimate conversation area is created by pulling all of the furnishings into the center of the room. A low table with modern lines allowed the creation an artistic vignette that offset the big expanse of the back of the sofa.

When you bring your furniture into cozy conversation areas, no matter the size of your room, you'll not only make your arrangements more attractive, but you'll more easily enjoy the family and friends you invite into the space.

Use Angling Judiciously

Angling furniture is all the rage, as well it should be, considering the way it can ignite a room with excitement and drama. If your room is small, however, you may not be able to take advantage of this bold technique because angling is *not* technically the best use of space. However, if I'm working with a client who wants to add pizzazz to his or her interior and doesn't own a lot of furniture, (and isn't inclined to purchase more), I always suggest angling the existing pieces. It fills the space, looks fashion forward, adds tremendous character, and doesn't require the addition of extra pieces.

Angling in the living room

In a living room, if you do opt to angle your sofa, ideally your large area rug should be laid on the same angle as the sofa it's "supporting." Place side chairs and a coffee table (or a tufted ottoman, another design rage) across from the sofa and the basic arrangement is complete. The one issue to watch when angling furniture is the possibility of sharp edges sticking out, which are called *silent arrows* in Feng Shui. I've bruised my thighs on many a silent arrow in my earlier days, so take care that all corners of angled tables or carved chairs don't jut out into the traffic corridors of the room.

We opted to break a decorating "rule" here by not facing the sofa toward the fireplace. We thought the sofa made a far more artistic statement facing outward, visible to all guests as they enter the space.

Angling in the bedroom

In a bedroom, an angled bed looks fabulous as long as you can live with the obvious adjustment: you won't have a wall to support your back. This is okay unless you don't have a headboard. According to the principles of Feng Shui, if you don't have a headboard, you need to compensate in some way so that you feel anchored and secure in your bed. Consider placing a sofa table or console behind your bed and decorate it with plants and/or artwork and photos. You can also place a real or faux tree in this space, as long as it's not looming over your head.

Angling in the dining room

Dining rooms look particularly striking when the furniture is angled, as long as space allows. For some reason, this is an edgier look than angling the furniture in living rooms and family rooms, perhaps because of the typical absence of soft furnishings in the average dining room. But it's worth trying out if your dining room is large and you don't have enough furniture to fill the space, or if you consider yourself an edgy trend-setter when it comes to interior design! Ideally, keep the center of the table in line with the dining room chandelier, if one exists. If you don't currently have a dining room area rug, now may be the time to purchase one, because angling the table and chairs definitely gives a harder feel to the room. You'll want the softness an area rug provides. Adding real or faux trees and lower shrub-type plants (such as a schefflera, a.k.a. Queen Island Umbrella Tree) will also soften the sharp edges of the angled room.

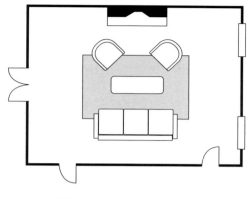

Whether or not you also angle the side pieces (china cabinet, console table, buffet, etc.) in your dining room depends on two factors: (1) Is there enough room to do so? You'll need adequate room to maneuver around your dining room table, and that usually means allowing at least two feet on all sides. If you find yourself bumping up against the drawers of a buffet or elbowing the glass door of your china closet, then no, you really can't afford to angle your side furniture pieces – they should be placed flush against the walls. And (2) how does it look? Angling your side pieces may look just too off-balance and disquieting, with all the hard furniture in the room placed at an angle. Try to intuitively "feel" the distinction in a room where edginess and tension (which are hip and good in interior design) crosses the line to feeling un-grounded and uncomfortable (not so good).

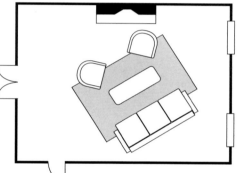

Notice how simply angling the furniture in a layout can infuse the space with excitement and interest; best of all, it brings good Feng Shui to the space!

The final consideration is where to put your area rug. I've seen rugs look good when they are angled along the lines of the dining room table and chairs. I've also seen area rugs look very interesting when they are *not* angled, but are placed parallel to the wall. When placed squarely in the center of the room, area rugs anchor the space, offering a nice balancing and stabilizing effect against the angled furniture.

Free up your energy
Aside from the obvious visual benefit of angling furniture, there's another great reason to consider angling your pieces. In the world of Feng Shui, it creates fire energy and movement that, particularly with bedroom furniture, can be wonderfully therapeutic for a stale or stagnant relationship. Here's to new beginnings!

Un-bulk Your Spaces

I was recently hired by a neighborhood mom who was daunted by her small (approximately 12x15-foot) family room. She had two toddlers and felt she would be considered a bad mother if she got rid of her big, puffy traditional sofa and chairs. She also felt she must keep her wall-to-wall carpet to maximize her children's crawling pleasure, despite the fact that it was worn and stained. To make matters worse, she had two dark-stained, chunky bookcases that flanked her two small windows, which were heavily dressed in cotton drapery panels and valances. Because there was no overhead lighting, she had three table lamps sitting on dark chunky end tables that matched a dark coffee table. Other than the worn carpeting, none of the pieces in the room were poor quality. They just didn't bring out the best in each other, especially in a small space.

You're probably getting a visual sense of how insulated and claustrophobic this room was; no wonder she was miserable and frustrated (sometimes clients wait too long before calling for help... Give yourselves a break, call a designer!) I gave her permission to un-bulk, to put her room on a diet. After walking through several scenarios and what each would cost, we decided on the most cost-effective ways of bringing the greatest change to this space.

For starters, we replaced the puffy sofa and chairs with streamlined pieces. In this case, steamlined meant the pieces had straight, not curvy, lines. The sofa and chairs had exposed legs instead of kick skirts and the two side chairs were armless. We removed the wall-to-wall carpet in favor of hardwood floors and added a soft area rug. We moved the chunky, dark bookcases downstairs; my client decided she didn't need any of the books they held, so she donated all of them to charity. For additional airiness, we removed the drapery panels, leaving only a top valance on each window, and mounted this valance higher up on the wall, just under the ceiling line, to allow more light to come in through the window.

The icing on the cake was my client's decision to have recessed lights installed. My husband being an electrician notwithstanding, recessed lights are one of the most attractive and functional investments you can make that will more than return your dollars when you sell your home. With the addition of the recessed lights, we were able to donate to charity all of the chunky end tables and the table lamps that sat on top of them. Finally, we replaced the wooden coffee table with a wildly popular leather ottoman. Its buttery-soft hide was as stunning as it was child-friendly.

This once small and crowded space not only looked less "bloated," but was reincarnated as a fresh, stylish, and bright family room fit for adults and toddling cherubs alike.

And remember, while this story was about a client with a small living room, this idea can apply to any room – large or small – that's generally overfilled with too much stuff! Even if your room is huge, if it's stuffed to the gills with furnishings, heavy textiles, and clutter, it will be crowded – so purge away!

What a fabulous example of an uncluttered, clean-lined space. The homeowners, who prefer a low-maintenance approach to home décor, opted against an area rug, kept accessories to a minimum, and let bold paint color on the walls do the talking.

When It Comes To Area Rugs, Size Matters

Area rugs are a creative and cost-effective way to inject new life to a tired interior. They are available in hundreds of patterns and almost as many price points. You can find them in exclusive rug boutiques, mid-range furniture showrooms, or even national superstores. With so many options available these days, you shouldn't have any trouble finding a rug that fits your style and budget.

Size

Let's discuss size – of rugs that is. Many clients are often befuddled by which size rug they should buy for a particular room. In the dining room, for example, many make the mistake of buying an area rug for under the table that's too small for the space. While you may have beautiful hardwood floors you want to show off, don't end up looking like you bought a large placemat for under your table! It's a good rule of thumb to purchase a rug that's at least two to three feet longer and wider than where the dining room chairs sit when tucked into the table. This way, even when you pull the chairs out, the back legs of the chair won't be off the rug. The end result looks lavish and not like you ran out of money and couldn't afford the larger size.

In master bedrooms, on the other hand, I tend to see the opposite tendency. Clients will purchase an area rug that completely fills the space, but two-thirds of the rug ends up hiding under the bed. If you splurge and buy a rug of some pedigree, that's a wasted investment, in my opinion. Runners and small area rugs will still afford you the creature comfort of sinking your feet into something warm and plush when you crawl out of bed, and you won't be wasting any of it under the bed. This will also make your cleaning easier if you have hardwood floors, since hard floors hold less dust than soft surfaces.

Using small area rugs, or runners, in your bedroom allows you the creature comfort of sinking your feet into warmth on chilly mornings and prevents you from wasting cash by not having the majority of a large area rug hidden under your bed.

Finally, in the living room or den, when you purchase an area rug to anchor a seating area, don't buy too much rug. Very often a 5x7-foot or 6x8-foot area rug is sufficient. An 8x10-foot rug often ends up under the couch and extending far beyond the edges of the chairs. Unless you have the square footage in a room to literally widen your seating area, stick with the smaller rug. In a living room or den, it's not necessary for *any* the feet of the furniture to be sitting on the area rug.

Price

I'm often asked, "What will I have to spend on a decent area rug?" I usually answer this question by giving clients three ranges to think about. Ultimately you will need to decide what portion of your design budget you want to dedicate to area rugs. There's no right or wrong answer; it's a purely personal decision. In my part of the country, here's generally what I tend to find:

• *High-end:* Imported wool and wool/silk blend rugs, found at rug boutiques or high-end furniture showrooms. An 8x10-foot rug can range from $5,000-$10,000, but many boutiques will negotiate price. Most boutiques will let you take home a few rugs to try out in your home before you buy, in exchange for a credit card number, so you can determine if the rug really works in your space.

• *Mid-range:* This category is really large. You can get a very attractive 8x10-foot wool rug for $1,500. You can also get one on sale, because it's last year's stock perhaps, at a furniture showroom for $500. You'll also find this price range in the national home décor catalogs. Keep in mind that some of these rugs may be machine-made rather than handmade, but it will still be one-hundred percent wool with a nice thick pile. You'll have to decide if a handmade rug matters to you – you'll pay extra for it.

• *Bargain range:* You can find synthetic rugs at national home-improvement stores or discount chains. For an 8x10-foot rug, you can pay as little as $150. You may be able to find these rugs in great colors and snappy patterns, so they are certainly a good option if you're on a tight budget. Do remember, however, that you get what you pay for: synthetic rugs are often thin, not plush, and their overall feel to the touch may be rough.

Note how this 8x10-foot area rug is large enough that the chairs still stay on it even when pulled out from the table.

As an alternate budget-minded option, look around in your area for stores that carry off-price or overstocked items at a steeply discounted price – they sometimes sell beautiful high-quality rugs for a song. In these stores, you'll regularly find 8x10-foot, one-hundred percent wool rugs for $200-$400, but you have to grab them quickly because they tend to be one-of-a-kind and can rarely be reordered. I'm sure there are stores like this in your area; it's worth finding them.

Area rugs are one of the most defining elements of an interior. They can single-handedly shift the design direction of a traditionally decorated space. On the other hand, a conservative area rug can balance the stimulation often found in artsy, wildly patterned, or eclectic interiors. They reduce noise in your home by absorbing sound and add instant warmth and grounding to a hard floor surface such as tile, cement, or wood. Despite what you ultimately decide to spend on an area rug, most rooms look better, more finished, with a rug than without one. Here's to sinking your tootsies into something comfy.

Jazz Up Broadloom With Area Rugs

Perhaps your broadloom is stained, outdated, or because you're renting, you don't have the option of replacing it. Area rugs placed directly over broadloom hide a multitude of sins and instantly refresh and update the room's décor.

Recently, I was hired by a couple to freshen up their home prior to the house going on the market. Their broadloom wasn't necessarily stained, but it was a bland beige tone with a very flat pile that definitely reflected the house's age. Rather than replacing the broadloom, we purchased several inexpensive wool blend area rugs and scattered them throughout the dining room, living room, and adjacent sunroom/den. The rugs were all different colors, sizes, and patterns but were connected in feel and tone. What a difference! The area rugs not only added splashes of color, but grounded the rooms in a way the bland beige broadloom never did. The rooms were transformed without having to replace the more costly pieces, such as the furnishings.

Ideally, place area rugs over low-pile carpet. If the area rugs tend to curl and won't lay flat, purchase inexpensive rug pads made of foam rubber that have a natural adhesive quality. You can buy rug pads specifically designed to adhere area rugs to broadloom, so you won't have to worry about tripping over any loose edges. Also remember that better-quality area rugs tend to be heavier, which means that they will be less likely to curl on you, which is especially important in high-traffic areas.

Oh, by the way, if you prefer the look of solids or neutrals, did you know you can have an area rug cut out from a piece of broadloom? Simply select a carpet you find appealing, provide accurate measurements, and the rug store will bind it for you. You'll have a custom-made area rug for significantly less than you'd pay for comparably-sized patterned area rugs. Want to add some pizzazz to the traditional décor of your living room? You don't have to totally redecorate the room. Along with some new pillows and a throw, new area rugs can instantly "contemporize" a tired traditional theme. Consider botanicals, abstract designs, geometrics, and of course, animal prints! And for the very fashion forward, have a look at the "new shag rugs" of the twenty-first century. They are different from the shags of the sixties (if anyone out there is old enough to remember them). The shag rugs of today are made from several types of yarns, curly and straight, and thus give a softer and more elegant look. You may also want to consider a leather shag area rug, which provides wonderful texture and dimension to any room. A shag area rug shows you have style and aren't afraid to walk on the edge just a bit!

This stunning wool rug inspired by the William Morris Arts & Crafts design style looks great on a hardwood floor. It could also easily cover a homely wall-to-wall carpet, reigniting the look of the room.

Shag is back with a vengeance! In this funky family room, a small shag area rug is used to punctuate the seating area. In this case, the area rug is not meant to hide the wall-to-wall carpet; in fact, the Berber is new. The black shag area rug looks crisp and striking against the merlot-colored Berber.

Chapter Six
Art and Accessories

Dress Your Artwork To Help It Look Its Best

I love art so much, there isn't an empty wall in any of my rooms. Some of my artwork is valuable; most is purely sentimental, but all are lovingly appreciated on a daily basis. If you haven't already graced your walls with some type of personal expression, there's no time like the present. While the art itself is always a very personal decision, there are many finishing details to consider that many of my clients get tripped up on – and the seemingly thousands of options in the framing stores don't help! If you take the time to consider the look you're after before you even step into a gallery or frame store, the process will seem much more manageable – and even fun!

While I do tend to favor oversized rather than undersized artwork on most walls, small artwork is used for effect in this space. The intentional use of diminutive frames virtually beckons you to step closer and peek in.

Choosing Art

Buy what you love. It's my experience that clients get overwhelmed over what they think should go in a space, rather than asking themselves, "What am I drawn to?" Other than the fact that I tend to think that a still life of fruit looks better in a kitchen or dining room than a bedroom, I always urge my clients to tell me what makes them feel good. Is it nature photography? Fine art prints? Ethnic art? Abstract art? Vintage posters? The list goes on and on. If you haven't already started to collect tear sheets from magazines of artwork that appeals to you, consider visiting a gallery or print/ frame shop. What isn't hung on the walls can be found in catalogs and large binders in the store. Ask to see the catalogs of available prints.

Should your artwork match your color scheme or contrast it? Not to be vague, but it really depends on your preference. Artwork "works" when it connects to the interior in some way. Sometimes that means the colors match. Other times it means the artwork is the only burst of color in an otherwise neutral room. In other cases, the artwork has a purpose or message. For example, on my office walls I hung three paintings I did when I was five years old. The colors don't particularly match my space, but the sentiment and inspirational quality of the paintings make them work wonderfully. In all of these instances the artwork relates to its interior and is successful.

I can tell you that according to Feng Shui, a successful room is one that is color-balanced in all of the elements. This means, for example, if your space is predominantly burgundy and burnt orange, which are hot, fire colors, you'll want to add the cool water quality of some blue somewhere – maybe in your artwork. Choose a piece of artwork that has both the fire reds and some cool blues; you may initially think the blues clash, but live with it for a while. Give yourself a chance to start to feel relief and comfort at the new balance of color.

Frames

I'm frequently asked if it's acceptable to mix frame styles in one room and the answer is absolutely! In today's design culture, almost any frame style and finish can coexist beautifully in one room, including antique brass, furry animal prints, forged and tooled iron, painted ceramic, and one of my newer favorites, jeweled Indian and mosaic glass frames – although you'll tend to find these picture frames in smaller sizes made for photos to be displayed on surfaces, rather than walls. While I lavishly use these varied frames to house my tabletop photos, when I'm hanging a collage on a wall, of like-themed photography, for example, I always rely on the stylish standby: matte black picture frames. They don't compete with the artwork and provide an elegant boundary around each special subject. Of course,

In our family room, I love displaying a riot of different picture frames and finishes all on one surface. It's the mix that makes it special.

many original paintings, as well as computer-generated reproductions, are available without any frame whatsoever. Instead, they're painted or reproduced on canvas stretched across a wooden frame. This is a more informal look – straight off the easel, if you will – and is perfectly acceptable in almost any décor setting.

Size

With artwork, bigger tends to be better. Erring on the side of oversized, rather than undersized, art for the space appears grand and stately. Too-small artwork appears stingy. This is especially true of artwork hung over a mantel or fireplace. Even if you plan on flanking a small print with candlesticks or other trinkets, to me, a too-small portrait over a mantel really sticks out like a sore thumb. How much wall above the mantel should you aim to cover? I try to have at least two thirds of the length of the mantel covered in artwork. This usually leaves more than enough room for you to place decorative objects to flank the artwork. Better yet, if you opt to hang a mirror over the fireplace instead of artwork, your end objects can encroach a bit, so they are actually reflecting in the mirror. This can look quite stylish.

Matting

Matting is the border that goes around a picture or print under the glass of the picture frame. It's usually made of cardboard covered in fabric, and is available in a multitude of colors. In general, matting adds elegance and a finished, professional touch to almost any artwork. While I've met gallery owners who disagree with this point (my local gallery owner was overheard saying with disgust at my choice of mats, "Those designers! Hmff!"), I think mats give you another opportunity to highlight the colors and subject matter in the piece (as opposed to using the perpetual white or beige mats, as they seem to prefer). For example, my husband and I recently purchased a giclee* called *Trois Amis* painted by local artist Michelle Kennedy. Ms. Kennedy, famous for painting pieces full of bright and bold colors, is an artist whose

Matching the larger mat to the color of the background walls allows this stunning female subject to dominate your attention, without competition or distraction.

A giclee is a digitally-produced high-fidelity reproduction scanned from an original piece of artwork; they are known for, among other things, their outstanding vibrancy. They combine the best of both original art and lithographs, and I highly recommend them!

style most resembles the lush strokes of Henri Matisse. Because our walls are painted in a faux finish of varying shades of cappuccino tan, we opted to surround the giclee with a double mat. The inner mat is midnight blue, which picks up some of the colors from the print, and the outer mat is tan, like our walls, but with a very thin gilded gold edging. The frame is also gilded an antique gold. The whole ensemble is absolutely striking on our tan walls. The subject matter just leaps out at you, and that's not just because the woman in the giclee is totally naked.

Ultimately, your choice of finishing details for your artwork is your call. The best way to decide how you'd like your artwork framed is to mosey over to the frame shop with your prints and photos; ask the clerk to lay out varying colors of mats and see what most appeals to you before you have your prints framed. You are the only one who can decide if you prefer a neutral matting or something brighter. As for me, what can I say: colorful people are attracted to all things colorful, including colorful mats. I feel no shame.

With Artwork, Plan First And Hang Second

Hanging artwork is particularly daunting to clients. Especially if you have freshly painted walls, or worse, freshly hung wallpaper – egad, this has to be perfect the first time! I can assure you that it *can* be perfect the first time, if you simply take the time to plan a little before you take hammer to wall.

Planning

If you have a piece or two to hang on a small wall, simply hold it up against the wall and see if it gives you the effect you're after. Do the colors work in the space? Does the subject matter contribute to the decor in some special way, whether it blends harmoniously or, conversely, does it add a nice contrast? Having the luxury of a second person available to hold up a picture while you stand back and observe is also infinitely helpful.

If you have a larger collection of pieces you want to hang in a group, consider placing them on a large bed, a table surface, or an open space on the floor. Lay out all of your pieces and think about what theme, if any, you want to express. For example, you may decide to hang all your black and white contemporary photography on one wall and all watercolors on another, while hanging all vintage family pictures on another wall. While eclectic decorating (mixing styles and décor genres) is terrific, most collections have far greater impact when grouped together, as opposed to being scattered all over the house (see Hanging Art in Groupings, page 72).

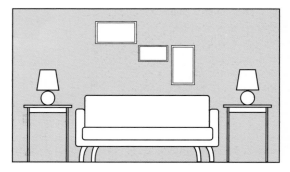 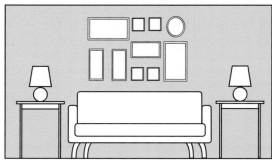

If you hang pictures with the future in mind, you can effortlessly build your collages over time, minimizing the need to start over every time you add a new picture.

Once the pictures are laid out on your trial surface, it's particularly helpful to have a Polaroid or digital camera available to capture the arrangement. Another tip: while the prints are still laid out on their trial surface, it's a good idea to roughly measure the overall length and width of the *entire* vignette. I've heard sad stories from more than one client of how they laid out an entire grouping on the floor, only to be disappointed when they ran out of wall space as they hung the prints. Make sure you have adequate wall space to execute your plan.

Arranging

What is the single most recurring faux pas I see in clients' homes? Art that's hung too high on a wall. Prints or portraits should be hung at approximately the eye level of a person standing between 5-foot 6-inches and 5-foot 8-inches tall. Of course, if you're a mostly diminutive family, I'm not advocating neck strain, so adjust accordingly. The goal is to be able to enjoy the artwork at a natural level.

If you're hanging prints of similar size on one wall, (such as a set of botanicals or a pair of contemporary abstracts) staggering prints on the wall tends to be a traditional look, while hanging prints horizontally across a wall on one plane is a more contemporary look. And while this point is debatable, if you opt to hang your prints of slightly different sizes in a modern fashion across the wall on one plane, I recommend lining up the bottoms, not the tops of the frames. To me, this is a more grounded, less "dangling" look than when you line up the tops of different size frames.

Hanging

So you've picked your collection of themed prints, you've identified which wall to hang which prints, and you know where on the wall you want your prints to go. How do you begin hanging them, you may ask? While my husband Steven seemingly takes six hours to measure every millimeter of space around and in between prints before driving the first nail, I on the

other hand tend to wing it. If I have a collection of, say, five to eight prints to hang, I decide which print will be my center focal point, hang it, and then I fill the entire space around the center print with all the others. Your center focal point can also be two large prints, while you "float" smaller prints all around them. I try to keep a similar amount of space between and among the prints, and hang all artwork in relation to each other, versus trying to spread them out across the wall.

We purposely created a step effect with these framed pictures in an attempt to bring your eye down in this slightly cavernous kitchen with nine-foot ceilings.

Displaying your art artfully isn't meant to stress you out or give you *agita*. Don't make it more complicated than it has to be. Well-placed art is another one of those design elements that elevates a room from nice to spectacular, even if your art is neither expensive nor significant.

Hanging pictures along the same plane gives these contemporary fabric squares just the right amount of modern clout. They nicely echo the horizontal trajectory of the banister.

Hang Framed Artwork In Relation To Each Other

Often I see artwork spread across an entire wall. This reminds me of strangers waiting at a bus stop – unrelated, anonymous, and distant. When hanging photos or pictures on a large wall, it's important that the artwork be hung close together (i.e. in relationship to each other) rather than spread across the entire wall. Even if you're hanging pictures over a couch or buffet, don't feel they have to spread over the entire seven-foot furniture piece. Try to have the pieces equidistant from each other, but centered over the middle third or half of the focal point, such as the couch or buffet. Especially if you're building a collage over time, by starting with a center cluster of pictures you can gradually fill the wall space around the cluster without having to take pieces down, patch holes, and start over.

If you have a small print you really love and must put it over a large area, such as the fireplace mantel, try to find a companion print or prints that will work with it as a group. They don't all have to be the exact dimensions, as long as they are related in some way, be it color or theme.

Also, feel free to add other accessories that aren't necessarily flat prints to the grouping. For example, several years ago I designed a Victorian bedroom with typically high ceilings, thereby leaving us with substantial wall space to fill. Along with three prints, we displayed a collection of small porcelain figurines that had one flat side, designed to be hung. On an opposing wall, we hung a Maxfield Parrish print and above it we placed a beautiful silk flower spray, with complimentary colors that matched the print. These additions can add a beautiful touch of the unexpected and transcend the ordinary definition of hung artwork.

Artwork is really one of those defining elements that elevates the overall sophistication of a space. Recently, while in the bedroom of two of my clients, they asked how we could spiff up the room for little or no money. Ah, do I love a challenge! Actually, this one was easy. The bedroom was painted a deep brick red and they courageously laid white linens on their bed.

The repetition of this black and white photography is what gives this display its excitement. Simple black matte frames also highlight the subject matter without competing; notice the punctuating pop of the red lampshade!

Over the bed, they had hung three large posters of differing themes and colors. The print in the center was a piece of black and white photography with a black matte frame. The ensemble was okay, but I knew it could be better. Luckily, I remembered that just outside the bedroom, along the beige hallway wall, there were several additional posters and photographs, again of differing colors and themes. So I switched two pieces of black and white photography from the hallway with the other posters from above the bed, and flanked the present black-and-white print in the bedroom. Voila! We suddenly had a striking trio of black and white photographs in black matte frames that looked magnificent on the brick red wall, against the white linens.

"Wow, we never thought to put these photos together on one wall," they exclaimed. That kind of statement is *always* music to my ears.

This elegant and formal dining room escaped looking heavy with the addition of an antique mirror. Both the dramatic window treatments and the glittery chandelier are reflected in this sphere of light.

Be Prudent With Your Use Of Mirrors

Most decorating novices know the benefit of placing a mirror in strategic places throughout your home. The more common places are over a fireplace mantel or hall table, ideally reflecting a pleasant view. (Which means if a mirror over your mantel reflects your hall closet – resist! Put a beautiful piece of artwork there instead.) Of course, consider adding a mirror on a wall that reflects windows; this instantly adds light and depth to any room.

Because mirrors are very powerful influences according to the principles of Feng Shui, there are places that are better served without the use of mirrors. The most obvious room where this is true is the bedroom. While it's customary to place a mirror over a bureau, bedroom mirrors can excite too much energy and interfere with restful sleep. If you aren't having trouble sleeping, then you don't need to change a thing. But if you do experience insomnia more than you think is average (in other words, you have trouble sleeping on a regular basis, instead of just when you're anticipating the excitement or stress of the next day), consider either removing the mirror or draping it with fabric when you sleep.

Two other places in the home where mirrors are inauspicious are the dining room and at the end of hallways. While the use of mirrors is considered de rigueur these days, if your dinner guests tend to eat and run, rather than linger and enjoy each others' company and conversation, you may want to consider removing the mirror from your dining room. And while design

What to do with a pesky empty corner? Bring love and life into it with family photos, faux greenery, and the vibrant energy only a mirror can impart. We adorned this one with dried hydrangeas from the client's own garden.

magazines often show mirrors on several walls in one room, the dining room isn't the place to experiment with this technique. According to the principles of Feng Shui, the mirrors might be stirring up too much Ch'i, and this energy could be preventing people from relaxing – also, many people just don't like to watch themselves eat! Additionally, I don't recommend putting a mirror at the end of a hallway. You run the risk of having a small heart attack every time you walk by and catch the glimpse of your own reflection and think it's an intruder.

Finally, pay attention to the type of mirrors you hang. Again, even though interior design magazines frequently display a collection of mirrors hung in a grouping on one wall, this isn't considered great Feng Shui either. When standing in front of it, you tend to see many broken-up images of yourself, which is unsettling and thus distorts the energy in the space. Ideally, pick mirrors that are one complete, unbroken piece of glass; beveling around the edges is fine. As long as their effects are considered carefully, mirrors can be a beautifully decorative and functional element in almost any room of your home.

Can you see the hanging cherubs fluttering across the wood molding of this whimsical bathroom window? A traditional fabric valance would have blocked all of the light, and not looked nearly as charming or innovative.

Why can't hung accessories be three-dimensional? These vibrant ethnic baskets give a modern appeal to this simple space while perfectly acknowledging the rich persimmon hue beneath the chair rail.

When Accessorizing, Try To Think Outside Of The Box

I know, this expression is so overused, but it's such a great concept. For example, when you think of window valances, don't limit yourself to fabric. In one client's traditional powder room, I hung her collection of painted pottery dessert plates over their window. In a country kitchen, over a small window above the sink, I hung dried hydrangeas from my garden and mixed them with a store-bought ivy garland and secured the piece with pushpins. Finally, for a couple who traveled extensively, I hung tribal masks over the windows in their library. A collection of almost anything, as long as it's "hang-able" looks great when it serves as a window treatment, especially if you have a small window that will be overdressed with standard draperies.

Once you get the hang of this, you can take it a step further. For a little boy who adored cowboys, I folded red western bandanas on an angle and ran a simple curtain rod through the top for his bedroom window. I also repeated this "valance" by sewing additional bandanas across the top of a store-bought blue plaid shower curtain, for a smashing "custom" look.

One of the hottest accessories today is the chandelier. Glittery crystals and hanging orbs are no longer seen only in ornate dining rooms. I've installed whimsical white iron chandeliers with glass flowers and painted berries in little girls' bedrooms and baths, and have hung an aged and tarnished brass chandelier in the corner of an eclectic salon, so it illuminates a couples' wedding portrait. Hanging chandeliers in atypical places adds instant elegance while expressing just a bit of design daring on your part!

Looking for inspired ways to use innovative accessories? See page 82 (Decorate with Loved Objects) and consider if you have a comparable collection of something as meaningful or sentimental as my client's string instruments. If you've traveled to the Far East, why not hang a stunning kimono across a piece of bamboo and mount it on your living room wall? Or, if you're an outdoorsman, try hanging your snowshoes and fishing rods on a large accessible wall. They will be beautifully displayed and still readily available when next the spirit moves you to trek in the fjords or snag a fresh catch.

Go ahead! Start foraging through your closets and attics, nooks and crannies. I bet there's something special just waiting to be unearthed and displayed in a unique way. You too can take your home from the expected to the highly innovative, with a beautiful, personal expression of you!

Simple dime-store bandannas added an authentic western flavor to this store-bought plaid curtain. We added the same bandannas to the adjoining window treatment (not pictured).

What's the easiest way to add glamour to your tired dining room? Hang a stunning glittery chandelier of course! This one is festooned in clear crystals, as well as amethyst and amber-colored orbs – simply divine!

Accessories Are Happier In Groups

When decorating any long or large surface, avoid lining up your accessories in an equidistant fashion – they will look like they are waiting in line to buy tickets to some event. Instead, make groupings, or what we designers call "vignettes," of odd numbers of items, ideally three.

For example, atop kitchen cabinets in a country kitchen, consider the following grouping: a wicker basket with faux ferns flanked by a French crock to its right and a handsome ceramic rooster to its left. Or in a contemporary living room, group a small (approximately 8x10-inch) painted canvas on a tripod with a statuette or bust on its right, and to the left, a beautiful vase. You get the idea? A trio of artistic objects becomes a visual feast when grouped together rather than standing alone.

Please make sure these chosen objects are similar sizes; you don't want the scale of the grouping to be inconsistent.

Recently I was asked to decorate a sports-themed family room. The inside shelves were easy, but what to put on top? We found a creative solution by hanging one of those long panoramic photos of Fenway Park above the center cabinet. Then we flanked the print on either side with a grouping of objects that were sentimental to the client. Believe it or not, one side held a very securely mounted bowling ball with antique duckpins surrounding it. The other side displayed a large antique wicker fish creel with a child-size fishing pole. Because each object was very large, we didn't necessarily need to add a third object in each vignette, yet the overall effect was balanced and was properly scaled.

Sometimes clients (and we designers!) can over-think design decisions. This small alcove just exudes style by virtue of its simplicity.

Grouping vignettes is an art to be sure, but can be accomplished with simple trial and error. Try to find some connection among the objects, such as a shared theme, e.g., country accessories or sports-related items. The objects can also be unrelated and just special to you, like the example given earlier with the painted canvas, the statuette, and the vase. I tell my clients to think of what a city skyline looks like (or for the TV buffs out there, the opening line drawing on the former hit show *Frasier*). It's the varying heights of objects that make the vignette interesting.

Also consider varying the texture and feel of objects in your vignettes. This can be done easily by mixing old and new pieces – aged items with a beautiful patina can happily co-exist with newer, refined objects. Everyone has his or her own tolerance for this look, so let your gut be your guide. If you like the look of shiny porcelain juxtaposed with an unfinished plaster plaque, wonderful. If the arrangement makes you happy, that's what's important. With a little practice, you too can become a skilled creator of the vignette!

How delightful to happen upon a small vignette or tablescape, as they are commonly known. Some pieces are antiques; others are found treasures from a flea market. But they happily coexist because their scale is similar and they are given adequate room to "breath." Remember, small vignettes are easily overshadowed by larger pieces, so group small objects together.

A collection of Italian pottery, faux fruits, and greenery nicely fills the open space above these cabinets, and again, brings the eye down from the nine-foot ceilings.

Treat Tall And High Surfaces With Respect

I often see very small objects placed on the top of kitchen cabinets or along the top of tall armoires and wall units. Not only does this make the tall furniture look silly, but it makes the small objects themselves appear unimportant. When you have to look up to view something, it automatically necessitates that those objects be of larger scale. A client once had her entire Lladro china collection on top of her seven-foot armoire because she felt they would be safe there. Unfortunately, no one ever noticed them up there in the skyline, given the fact that each figurine was only six to ten inches tall. So for starters, we put her valuable collection in a lighted china cabinet she purchased specifically for them, so they could be viewed from eye level (and therefore appreciated). Then we decorated the armoire with substantial objects such as large baskets, crocks, and a decorative birdcage that could be seen easily from the floor.

Kitchen cabinets deserve the same treatment. While wicker and rattan baskets seem to be the easiest item to collect en masse above your cabinets, pay attention to the size of basket you choose to display. Even several baskets will look unimportant sitting on a high surface if they're only five or six inches in diameter. In this case, quantity doesn't make up for lack of size. Instead, purchase very large and substantial baskets. Consider sitting them on their side and filling them with papier mâchè or faux fruit and greenery spilling out of them.

If your cabinets have those pesky uneven surfaces, where your cabinet moldings and doors are higher than the top surface of the cabinet, fear not. An old trick is to build up the top of the kitchen cabinet with old magazines, phone books, or plastic containers, then place your decorative objects on these props. Just make sure the footing is secure and the weight of the object is evenly distributed. Or, for a more permanent solution, consider fitting sheets of plywood or MDF (multiple-density fiberboard) to the openings (or having a handyman do it for you). That way, you won't have to worry about rearranging stacks of phone books every time you want to rearrange your accessories. Either way, by building up the space below your accessories, you'll be able to see the objects, and not just the top parts.

By making an effort to acknowledge the special decorating considerations high surfaces require, you'll avoid a common decorating dilemma. You'll be able to better see, and therefore enjoy, larger accessories placed on high surfaces, and never need to break out the binoculars.

Faux greenery and baskets 'a plenty are the easiest way to add decorative emphasis to tall surfaces. Take them down a few times a year and sprinkle them under the shower to keep them looking alive, so to speak.

While this client's vanity functioned as her makeup table, we took great care to display items as if they were pieces of art. A lavender boudoir lamp from the thirties, a decoupage tissue box from the fifties, and silk corsages from the forties: this sweet area in her bedroom is all about nostalgia. Every morning my client got to sit here and preen – what a lovely way to begin each day.

Decorate With Objects That You Love

This idea may seem incredibly obvious, yet I often meet clients who are sadly enslaved to fashion, whether it's what they wear or how they feel they should decorate their homes. These folks think they have to entirely redecorate their homes every few years to keep up with the current trends. While the businesswoman in me says, "Way to go, let's get started!" my voice of reason wonders why they have tired of the beautiful interior we just finished not that long ago. So instead of following the fickle whims of trends, consider using objects that are personally meaningful to you, regardless of the current hot style.

In my first year as a designer, I met a woman who knew the value of sentimental objects; I certainly had something to learn from her. While gazing at a bowl of wax fruit in her kitchen, I foolishly suggested that we should "ditch this" and replace it with something more updated and stylish. She recoiled with horror, and rightfully so. I was talking about throwing out her Nana's wax fruit from the fifties. The fruit symbolized countless lazy days at Nana's house, eating Stella Doro cookies and drinking milk at the kitchen table. That day I learned two valuable lessons: (1) Never assume anything and (2) decorate with the objects you love, unequivocally. So to rapidly salvage my failing reputation, I rummaged through my client's cupboards and picked the prettiest porcelain bowl I could find. I nestled her Nana's wax fruit in a bed of Spanish moss and silk ivy gratefully borrowed from her crafts room, giving it a new life in all its vintage glory.

I'm reminded of another client who lived in a third floor apartment of a beautiful 1800s Brownstone in Salem, MA. He had a very long narrow hallway that was difficult to decorate; he wanted to do something more original than hang a row of gallery-type prints. We foraged through his closet and, lo and behold, found a wonderful collection of his grandfather's antique string instruments: a lute, a mandolin, a ukulele, and more that I can't even pronounce. We hung them all, one exquisite piece of carved wood after another, in the hall. This long, hard-to-decorate hallway became a hallowed hall from his past, where he could gaze at the instruments or take them down to pluck and strum to his heart's content.

Living with objects that are meaningful, despite their worn or old appearance, has been popular with the Japanese for centuries. In fact, their philosophy, called **wabi-sabi**, is gaining new acclaim in the Western design world, helped in part by the success of Feng Shui, as Westerners are (finally!) beginning to realize the benefits of these wonderful Eastern philosophies. Wabi-sabi isn't necessarily a style, but more an aesthetic with a subtle spiritual component. In his book *Wabi-Sabi for Artists, Designers, Poets and Philosophers*, author Leonard Koren defines wabi-sabi as "the beauty of things imperfect, or incomplete, modest or humble."

They say that jewelry can be considered wearable art. This jewelry is also considered displayable art to this client! This photo features some of her favorite dangly earrings. We both thought they were far too pretty to be stored away in a jewelry box. The hours of viewing pleasure will far outweigh the occasional dusting you'll have to endure should you decide to display your favorite jewels.

Wabi-sabi actually transcends interior design; in fact, it encourages a lifestyle that brings a sense of hospitality and peace not only to your home, but to your life. For the interior design community to finally see a connection between spirituality and the most precious place we call home – I say it's about time!

What's Old Is New Again!

"Shabby Chic" emerged a few years back as an unexpected yet appealing design style. In her books, "Shabby Chic" creator Rachel Ashwell offers countless ways to bring the relaxed and comfy feel of her characteristically aged style to your home. Think of "Shabby Chic" as the antithesis of the refined English manor style. In fact, it's epitomized by scuffed-up surfaces, slouchy cushions, and time- and weather-worn artifacts.

The use of architectural objects seems to transcend all decorating styles. While this dining room is decidedly French in feel due to the French provincial chairs and busy floral patterns on the walls and seat cushions, the Greek Ionic columns blend seamlessly with the décor.

I know this style doesn't appeal to all people. My own mother once said, while looking at a bureau I was picking out for a client, "I grew up with scratched and beat-up furniture – why would anyone pay for these now?" Many prefer a less aged, more gentile, sensibility to their furnishings and accessories. Yet, I'm here to tell you that many interiors lend themselves to even just a touch of this Old World style of accessorizing. Incorporating just a few architectural elements or relics from the past just might add the character you never knew your space was missing!

For example, many traditional interiors would welcome the addition of standard garden ornaments typically designed for the yard. Consider placing a graceful figurine of an angel or a heron next to an overstuffed chair in the den, beside the magazine basket. Add authentic weathered birdhouses to a sunroom, either hung on a wall or sitting on a console or coffee table. Even a Gentlemen's library with adjoining humidor would look smashing with the addition of an antique croquet set or aged dartboard from the forties.

Hmm, where have we seen this bust before? I think the buzz word these days is to "repurpose"! This once-regal bust of the Greek god Antinous met an untimely death at the hands, or should I say paws, of running felines. He has now been repurposed as beautiful garden art amongst my petunias and phlox.

I recently worked with a client who was enamored with the Neo-Classical style, which is a formal style characterized by Greek and Roman design motifs – the pedestal being the most recognized – calm and pale colors, and elegant symmetrical furnishings.

She was concerned however, that this style can look a bit stuffy; she sought to make it just a bit less staid, more inviting. The clear solution was to add the weathered patina of authentic architectural elements such as fencing grates, freestanding columns, and a collection of finials and newels on some of her surfaces. The juxtaposition of the elegant furnishings and the unadorned accessories was the perfect antidote to the potential stuffiness.

Finally, the cottage/beach style is totally at home with worn and weathered additions. Imagine building a privacy screen out of three or four chipped and painted louvered doors that have been hinged together. In one of the beach houses I owned, I had a very old and distressed oil painting of a harbor hanging over the living room sofa. In the master bedroom, I clipped my collection of vintage silk flowers to the corners of my lace café curtains. And in the guest bedroom, a pair of painted still-life prints from the forties danced across a sidewall, abutted by a very fetching dress form from 1952, the year my true love was born! That, to me, is personality!

Chapter Seven
Fabric Treatments

Fill Your Home With Fabulous Fabric!

You know you should be an interior designer when you would rather hang out in a fabric store than go to a movie. When I was a child, I used to collect scraps of wrapping paper. I would cut them into small pieces and make mosaic scenes out of them. Or sometimes I would just accumulate them, spread them out on the kitchen table, and gaze at them as if they were hundred-dollar bills. The patterns and colors were magical to me. It wasn't until I was eleven years old, in Home Ec. class, that I discovered the wonder of fabric and learned how to sew. This was when fabric trumped the marvel of wrapping paper.

This family room is all about bold color and fanciful fabrics. The leopard print can hold its own in a mélange of purple, claret, and butternut yellow fabric. A riot of colorful toss pillows don't overwhelm because they're essentially solid in tone, albeit trimmed in beads and tassels.

As I mentioned in my Introduction, some of my female clients are often embarrassed because they don't feel they have the natural propensity to decorate their homes (in actuality many of them have wonderful taste and instincts; it's the confidence to act on it that they lack). They literally break out in a sweat at the thought of entering a fabric store and having to choose something from the thousands of options. Yet fabric is one of the single most defining elements of any space. As I discussed on page 26, Mixing Patterns and Prints, a fabric's personality is defined not only by its color and pattern, but by its "feel" and mood. Demystifying the world of fabrics is one of the most empowering lessons I can impart to my clients. Similar to my fourth grade teacher telling me, "Jayne, long division is our friend," I try to help my clients overcome their Fear of Fabric and embrace its many wonderful benefits.

On page 58, Un-bulk Your Space, I actually discussed a room that had too many textiles in it. It felt stuffy and bloated and needed more hard surfaces to shine through. More often, however, I enter rooms that need the magic of fabric to soften the edges, insulate against cold and echoes, and generally impart wonderful color and personality to the space.

Aside from the usual places we hang fabric (windows), I like to suggest to clients that they consider some non-traditional ways in which fabric can be their friend. Did you know that before wallpaper was invented people used to glue fabric on their walls? And remember tapestries hanging on cold, drafty castle walls from your studies of medieval history? Even some wallpapers that are particularly patterned or have a raised nap can function as fabric in a room. Visually they fill in the room, and physically they insulate against cold and noise.

Why not take a gorgeous piece of fabric and stretch it over canvas panels to be hung as artwork? This looks particularly hip with abstracts and mid-century inspired "mod" patterns. I like the look of three large canvases in a row, or four smaller canvases hung in a box formation.

I once worked with a client who wanted to hang a Mexican sombrero (a beloved honeymoon souvenir) on her family room wall. It looked good there, but the wall was large and something was missing. I got the idea to hang a Mexican serape (blanket) on the wall and sort of drape it into place with tacks. I then hung the sombrero over the backdrop of the serape. This more completely filled in the wall space and the black velvet sombrero looked stunning against the gorgeous deep hues of the serape.

If you're fortunate enough to live in a home with a large and spacious master bedroom, you know that sometimes it's a challenge to fill in this space and minimize a potentially cavernous feeling. I worked with a couple who really wanted a stunning and exotic romantic haven in their large bedroom. So in addition to purchasing substantial pieces of furniture to fill the space, I suggested we cover the entire wall behind their king-size bed in gathered fabric. We chose a very soft flowing jersey knit and triple-gathered it across the entire wall. Their king-size headboard looked majestic against this treatment, and here's the fun part: there was a small annoying window on this wall that got covered along with everything else. There were enough other windows in the room so covering it wasn't a problem. We took a negative and turned it into a positive with the help of fabulous fabric! You can use this treatment in any room in your house; bedrooms do, however, lend themselves particularly well to the luxurious effect of draped fabric.

Even a little window over the kitchen sink deserves special attention. Here we used two fabrics that weren't created as coordinates but fit the bill supremely. The red, yellow, and green plaid shade shared the same deep tones as the red gathered valance; the red valance was covered in little yellow speckles that perfectly matched the yellow in the striped fabric. With so many matching tones, this ensemble works like a charm.

A final interesting and unusual application for fabric is to use it in lieu of a wall. We've all seen how fabric room dividers offer the necessary privacy or boundaries a long or large room require. But imagine you have a very obvious stairway emptying out in your room (found often in townhouses) that seemingly acts as a funnel, visually drawing you into its gaping opening. By running a track along the ceiling and hanging sheer fabric along the side of the stairway banister you have, in effect, built a soft wall that blocks off the unsightly view of the stairs. The trick is to select a fabric that's the same color as the surrounding walls so it appears to be an extension of the wall. The stairs are now less dominant and your eye is drawn into the center of the room, not at the eyesore stairway.

Use your imagination; I bet you too can come up with creative and innovative ways to use fabric and be the envy of all of your neighbors.

More On The Joys Of Fabric

So now I've hopefully helped you overcome your Fear of Fabric. You now understand that fabric is not only the visual icing on the cake of a room, but it insulates against both noise and cold. So now you're probably wondering, how do I begin selecting fabrics? This is as daunting as hanging artwork, right? It doesn't have to be. Many clients have already seen something they like, be it in a store window or in a magazine. Start to take note of your surroundings – which colors and textures would you like to surround yourself with? Once you've identified the main fabric, as we discussed on page 26, Mixing Patterns & Prints, consider *not* playing it safe by adding only solid color fabrics as your coordinates. Window treatments and bed linens that are made of two and three coordinating fabrics (including prints, stripes, and florals, for example) immediately elevate a room from nice to spectacular.

Doesn't every interior benefit from a few feathers? For the faint of heart, start small by adding just a touch of feathers to places like lampshades and throw pillows.

For example, if you're doing your master bedroom, choose a primary fabric you truly love and consider using it as your main bedding fabric (duvet or bedspread) and as the main fabric for your window treatments. Select a second fabric and use this fabric for the dust ruffle, perhaps for the rosettes on your window treatments, and as the center panels of your pillow shams. Choose a third coordinate and use it for the outer flanges of the pillow shams, on a few throw pillows, and possibly as the fabric borders of your window treatments. There's no rule around what you should use where, only that you should love all three fabrics and that they coexist beautifully.

Make sure that you love the primary fabric enough to be seen in such a large expanse as your bedcovering or your living or dining room draperies. If your main fabric is a very bold and noisy print and you thus feel your coordinates need to be solid fabrics so the room won't feel too busy, at least consider a moiré, a nubby silk, a jacquard, or another type of tone-on-tone fabric. The subtle texture will be significantly more interesting than a flat solid fabric but won't compete with the main fabric or visually clutter up the space.

Go a step further and add embellishments. On the valances you can add trims such as fringe or tassels, or go a little more exotic with glass beads. If you fancy the authentic tribal look, consider adding piping made of little wooden bars or beads made of wood and cork. On the bottoms of your draperies, why not add a thick fringe of yarn called bullion fringe for a sexy, turn-of-the-century look. While you're at it, use a hot glue gun to add a foot or so of feather trim to the bottom of your boudoir lampshade. It may sound extravagant, but a touch of feathers provides just enough drama without overwhelming the space, and can be used in almost any décor. This is your bedroom! Why not be simply divine?

A formal and dramatic dining room deserves nothing less than spectacular draperies. For embellishments, we added a twisted silk cording along the top of the valance and lush fringe tassels along the bottom edge of the valance and the side panels.

Vintage Fabrics: What's "New"

Back in the early nineties, I was visiting a friend who lived in historic Salem, MA. On the way home, I couldn't resist stopping into one of the many wonderful antique shops that are dotted along the downtown commerce area of this lovely town. In my field, you can always justify popping into a new store, even if you should be heading to the gym, or worse, heading back to your office to your computer. I call these reconnaissance missions, and I rationalize that my clients expect nothing less from me...

Anyway, in one of the shops I happened upon a gorgeous bolt of robin's egg blue cotton fabric. It was covered in a riot of raspberry, pink, and burgundy flowers with soft green leaves and stems. The fabric was clearly from the forties, with that characteristic sheen. I had no idea what I was planning to do with it, but for $14 for the entire bolt, it was coming home with me.

About a year later, I ended up making very simple café curtains out of some of the fabric for a vintage fifties kitchen I was designing. Four years after that, I used the balance to cover a long window seat cushion and matching throw pillows in what I later coined an "eclectic salon" I was designing. The fabric added a pop of color and pattern to the mostly solid-toned room. The fabric was just so special and got compliments by all who set eyes on it. The irony is that fabric manufacturers are recreating these vintage designs of the forties and fifties, and are charging anywhere from $50-$150 per yard. What a gift to have found the "genuine article" for a pittance!

Half of me wants to tell you to keep your eyes peeled for such treasures because passing them by almost always haunts you. The other half of me, who just wrote a chapter on decluttering your spaces and resisting being a pack rat, says "No, don't!" I feel like I'm in that eighties movie where Dom Deluise has the angel on one shoulder and the devil on the other, both imploring him to do as they say! There's no easy answer, but one of my personal guidelines as to whether I should "buy or pass" has to do with the cost of the item. Small expenditures are easier to donate down the road if you don't end up finding the perfect use for that treasured buy.

Vintage fabrics

So let's talk a moment about the perfect use, or at least some creative uses, of vintage fabrics. Vintage actually describes a rather large category of patterns from the past. Most of you probably recognize vintage fabrics as those wonderful fanciful patterns of fruit and vegetable prints from the forties

In addition to the precious kitty named Winston, notice the café curtains made from that fabulous vintage fabric scooped up at the Salem antique store. This is the consummate fifties kitchen replete with vintage fabric, the colors red and blue, and especially the chrome table with vinyl seat cushions.

and fifties. These were the patterns most often utilized in the kitchen as tablecloths, dishtowels, and curtains. Yet there are many, many fabrics and patterns from yesteryear that make fabulous design statements in current décor. For example, the floral pattern I discovered in the antique shop in Salem was a formal, elegant pattern that was probably used not only to make home textiles but to make dresses and blouses worn by the stylish ladies of that era. You can also find a whole genre of vintage fabrics that are reminiscent of the glamorous era of Hollywood in the forties, adorned with grand banana leaves and lush orchids. A friend of mine found a whole bolt of this type of vintage fabric at the Brimfield Fair in western Massachusetts one year. It was woven cotton, and it had a certain heft to it, so rather than make curtains out of it that wouldn't necessarily drape smoothly, she decided to reupholster the cushions of her bamboo porch furniture with it – simply smashing!

And the last category of vintage fabrics I want to mention are the large group of fabrics that fall into the garment category. I know you've seen them. Men are wearing reproductions of bowling shirts and shirts from the *American Graffiti* era these days. Imagine a men's suit from the forties; it has a very distinctive, sometimes graphic pattern – picture a Zoot Suit! These would be examples of vintage garment fabrics.

Antique fabrics
Another category of period fabrics is the faded florals from the early 1900s – which are technically antiques, not vintage, because their style dates back more than one hundred years. This category is often called "tea-stained fabrics" because, due to their natural aging, they have acquired a sepia tone, which resembles fabric that has been dipped in steeped tea. Ralph Lauren popularized this antique cottage style in his bed linen collection a few years back.

Using vintage fabrics
While many people could easily envision using the fruit and vegetable vintage patterns as window treatments and throw pillows in a cottage style decor, I urge you to consider vintage fabrics in a larger sense when you're deciding on how to translate style into your interiors. You need not be creating a solely vintage vibe to justify using vintage fabrics. Very simply, vintage fabrics are cool and hip and can stand alone as a design element in a room. I've used them when designing funky, edgy spaces for clients who don't want a particular "look," rather they want more of a free-flowing artistic sensibility that looks more spontaneous than planned.

Also be on the lookout for more than just bolts of vintage fabric – pieces of vintage clothing are just as fun and useful! Imagine buying an old dinner jacket from the forties (that Zoot Suit mentioned above) and turning it into chic pillows for your mid-century sofa? Or as I mentioned on page 87, stretching cut fabric pieces from a vintage Hawaiian shirt over several canvasses and mounting them on the wall over the fireplace for a striking art display?

Whether you choose the kitchen florals, the lush and sexy tropical prints, or any of the fabrics used by the forties garment industry, vintage fabrics are hot and fashion-forward and can be found everywhere these days. I find them at yard sales, flea markets, used clothing stores (often much cheaper here), and, of course, antique shops. And before you spend a penny, ask your mother and aunts if there are any boxes lying around their attics, possibly filled with the very vintage linens you grew up with, assuming you're as old as I am and grew up with vintage linens!

And you thought I was writing fiction. Lo and behold, in the attic we found Nana Rossi's kitchen valance from the fifties. I think this will make wonderful throw pillows for my Cape house (and yes, Cousin Linda, I will share some fabric with you!).

Let Custom Treatments Improve Your Décor

Whenever I sit down with a new client, I always ask them what kind of budget they have put aside for the design project we're about to begin. *Very* often, clients will say they don't have a budget, which makes sticking to a budget infinitely harder! I know they say this because they're afraid that the designer will spend all of their money, so this way, if we're clueless as to what they have to spend, we can't spend it, right? It makes no sense to me either, but this happens very frequently. And you all thought this job was a piece of cake, eh? Anyway, with or without a budget figure, at every step of the design process I'll typically offer clients high-range, mid-range, and bargain options for all items. Some clients know they want to spend a good chunk of their change on an Oriental carpet, others prefer original artwork; whatever their preference is, it's fine with me. Whenever possible, however, I'll recommend that my clients consider spending some of their budget on custom window treatments and/or bed linens.

Custom fabric treatments are not inexpensive, but they are worth every penny. You'll have an infinite number of style options and a plethora of luscious fabrics from which to choose. I realize that you can certainly purchase affordable "bed-in-a-bag" type linen sets at many linen retailers – I've bought many myself for clients. Yet even the designer versions that cost upwards of $400 a set will still have their dust ruffle machine-surged, and not fully lined. They also tend not to have the beautiful embellishments around their shams, like double welting or contrasting fabrics in the center panels. If your budget allows, and the room is important to you, buy the most expensive linens you can afford – without a doubt, the extra money you invest will show.

A master bedroom is turned into an exotic and romantic retreat with the combination of custom linens and animal print accents.

Custom window treatments and a matching seat cushion bring a tidy sophistication to this unexpected little nook. Tassles on the valance and cording on the cushion edges add even more custom detail. And Daisy approves.

You can also opt for a combination: going the custom route *in conjunction* with store-bought pieces. For example, a few years ago, I designed custom window treatments and an upholstered headboard for the bedroom of my client's twelve-year-old daughter. All of the bed linens and pillows, however, were purchased from a catalog that specializes in teen bedroom linens and furnishings. By selecting coordinating fabrics for the headboard and window treatment, the end result was fun and sassy and looked like it was an entirely custom job.

Where should I have these custom linens made, you may ask? Most fabric stores offer custom work in addition to reupholstering services. Of course, most interior design studios that have a retail presence (open to the public) will probably specialize in window treatments and custom bed linens. In my town, even paint and rug stores have gotten into the custom arena. Some offer a limited menu of fabric choices and window treatment styles. Others have established a small fabric center in the back of the store where your fabric options can be quite plentiful, as well as the options for window treatment styles. Finally, many interior designers such as myself would be glad to do "just windows" for a client. It may not be the least expensive way of getting the project done, however, because some of us charge hourly, as well as for the labor and material costs to produce the end result. Yet, one of the benefits of working with a designer, and not a retail store, is that a good independent interior designer should show you any and all fabric choices you want to see, not just the ones carried by a paint or rug store. Because they may charge hourly, they simply have no incentive to be in a hurry the way many retailers are. They won't rush in and out of your home; rather they will spend the necessary time with you to really customize a look that's fitting to your interior.

So remember: In window treatments, as in life, you get what you pay for. Custom linens elevate your space from nice to spectacular. Aren't you worth it?

Window Treatments: The Final Frontier

Last Saturday I met a new client. She had a very pretty, tastefully decorated home with one exception: there was not a curtain or window treatment of any kind anywhere. When I asked her why, she replied, "Because I hate them." I chuckled out loud, taken aback at her revulsion of an inanimate and typically harmless object as a curtain. She is not unlike many clients I've met, however, who have hit the proverbial brick wall in the design process when it comes to curtains, or what we designers like to call in our best Mrs. Howell voice, "window treatments." Let me see if I can make this really easy.

Think of it this way: There are essentially three types of soft window treatments, that is to say those that are made of fabric. There are draperies. There are shades. And there are valances, a.k.a. "toppers." The rest are all variations on those themes.

Valances

I love valances. There are so many wonderful variations on this theme of window dressing, and in the last fifteen years or so, valances have been mass-produced and readily available in retail channels. You can find them gathered, scalloped, double-layered (as if they have a slip underneath), or made with points in the middle (with or without a tassel hanging from the point)! What seems to be the most common form of valance I see in homes? Swags and jabots. The swags and jabots treatment utilizes both a valance and a drapery; it's just that the drapery is highly abbreviated. Swags and jabots are also easily found in retail stores, but I urge you to look outside of the box and consider other options that are more unusual or less expected (sorry if I just offended anyone…).

Kingston and regal valances tend to be a bit more formal, where mock roman, pennant, and multiple point valances tend to be more casual, sometimes whimsical or playful. But as you know, the fabric you choose really determines what the final look will be.

A note of clarification: When you have valances custom made by a workroom or retail shop, very often the fabric will be mounted on a board, as opposed to hung on a standard curtain rod. Board-mounted valances always look more professional and substantial than those purchased to sit on a curtain rod, so don't be surprised when the workroom quotes you a substantial price.

Striking box pleat valances add drama and definition to this breakfast nook, which intentionally features no other accessories.

And speaking of soft treatments that have hard "insides," let me mention two other types of window treatments that technically fall under the soft window treatment category: cornices and lambrequins. Cornices are simply box-like structures that are made of wood and fastened across the top of the window. They are considered soft treatments because they are typically covered in fabric, although they can also be painted and stenciled with a design. For our purposes, they fall into the valance category, since they visually have the same effect. They aren't readily found in stores and are usually a custom-made treatment. Cornices can stand alone on the window, but are usually designed with matching draperies to be hung underneath. Lambrequins are simply cornices that completely frame the window on three sides. Both cornices and lambrequins tend to be formal and regal treatments, especially the latter.

Draperies

Draperies are what many of we Baby Boomers grew up with. The variations on this theme are pinch pleat drapes, rod pocket drapes, and tab-top curtains. Draperies are the most popular store-bought treatments you'll find. Most store-bought drapes won't be lined, which means they might be flimsy and may let in more light than you want, so shop wisely. You may decide to go the custom route, as we discussed on the previous page, to get just what you want.

Let me digress for a moment to illustrate a point about draperies. When puddling drapes (which are so long the extra length of the fabric "puddles" on the floor) hit the scene a few years back, everyone was adding sumptuous pools of fabric everywhere. I remember walking into a kids' playroom where formal curtains were puddling on the floor... Or should I say that was the mother's intent. In actuality, between the kids and the dog, some of the curtains were dragged across the floor, while the once-softly draped scarf above was wrapped tightly over the curtain rod, desperately clinging to life. Lesson: Dress your rooms appropriately for their purpose. Puddling drapes are one of the most formal window treatments; hanging them in a kid's cluttered and raucous playroom is an instant recipe for disaster. This playroom had one large bay window facing the front of the yard and two smaller double-hung windows on the side wall. All of these windows would have been much more appropriately dressed in valances, forgoing the side panels that are a sure temptation for a game of juvenile hide and seek.

In her cozy bedroom, this client liked the look of layered window treatments and preferred her drapes stop at the windowsill.

Puddling drapes are almost always formal and elegant. Save these for your living and dining rooms, or perhaps your dramatically decorated master bedroom. Drapes that graze the floor can be formal or casual depending on the fabric. Obviously a nubby silk or jacquard drapery will scream luxury more than a gingham plaid cotton drapery. Tab-top curtains are usually more casual than rod pocket or pinch pleat drapes. And drapes that stop at the windowsill tend to look the *most* informal and, dare I say, a bit dated.

And speaking of dated (I hope my aunts don't smack me for this), tiebacks – unless they are silky ropes, or made of wrought iron, metal, etc. that screw onto the wall – also look a bit dated, or at the very least, very conservative. If you want to tie back your panels, choose a fabric that has a nice soft texture and allow enough yardage so the folds are full and soft, not tight. Personally, I usually like the drapes to meet in the center of the window if you're going to use tiebacks – the exception being if you use drapes and tiebacks on a large bay window; then you want to make sure your exposed center curtain rod is pretty enough to be seen. With respect to privacy, draperies can be made to be functional, that is to say they are wide enough to fully cover the entire width of your window when drawn closed, or ornamental, where they are designed to be stationery all of the time and offer no privacy, just good looks!

Wrought iron tie-backs such as these are readily available in home decorating stores everywhere. Consider adding a matching curtain rod with finials for a striking, pulled-together look.

Austrian shades in a purple and celadon puckered silk stripe add elegance to the newly renovated spa retreat.

Shades

There are essentially two types of fabric shades: the puffy versions such as Austrian shades, balloon shades, or cloud shades; and the tailored versions such as Roman shades. You might be able to find the occasional balloon shade in retail stores; you definitely can find them in linen catalogs. I've even started to see versions of Roman shades in national home décor department stores, but they are made in a limited selection of dimensions, so they may not fit your windows. If you want your fabric shades to truly coordinate with your furnishings and linens, again, you know what I'm going to say, right? Have them custom made.

Austrian, balloon, and cloud shades are full and voluminous and look lovely in formal settings. They require a good deal of fabric, so they aren't the least expensive custom treatment you can order. Roman shades, on the other hand, are tailored and streamlined, and tend to look either more casual or more contemporary than other styles, depending on the fabric. Having said that, I once designed Roman shades in a gorgeous embroidered silk, and added glass beads as trim. These were clearly formal. All fabric shades are technically difficult to make, so a workroom will charge accordingly, but well-made fabric shades are worth the investment. It will be obvious that you put some serious money into your windows. Remember, however, that as attractive as fabric shades are, they essentially offer two options: opened and closed. If you're looking for light filtering options, you'll find more choices with hard window treatments.

A final word on fabric shades: make sure you're okay with having the rings and cords visible through the window to the outside world. They cannot be concealed with lining, so if you think these elements will ruin your house's curb appeal, you may want to consider other window treatments.

Choosing a style

"How do I know which style is the right treatment for my room," you ask? Well the first consideration is preference. Do you like the look of valances versus draperies? Some people just prefer the more heavily-dressed look that draperies provide. Others use both: draperies and a decorative valance of some sort across the top of the window.

The other practical considerations are as follows:

• Do you have small windows? If so, draperies may dwarf them even further, unless you hang them above and beyond the window moldings (discussed in detail on page 137).

• Will you be placing large furniture such as a sofa under these windows, thereby blocking the bottom half of the draperies?

• Is there a significant heat source that will be blocked or covered by the draperies?

• Is the room fairly small? If so, again, yards and yards of drapery fabric will further accentuate the diminutive dimensions of the room.

• Do you have a very wide, but short (6x2-foot, for example) bank of windows you're trying to dress, characteristic of some ranch houses built in the fifties? If so, long draperies will frankly look odd on this type of window.

Of course, you can keep the room light and airy by hanging valances with sheers under them. This is still a lighter look than draperies, and provides a bit of privacy, if that's important to you.

Admittedly, there are a lot of details involved in window treatments, but if you try to remember the three basic categories, you'll most likely eliminate what doesn't work for you and easily envision the window treatment that does.

Window Treatments: The "Hard" Facts

Hard window treatments have metal or wood built into their construction. Very often I'm asked by clients, "Should I put cellular shades on my windows? How would shutters look? Is this too much dressing for one window?" Before I list the various types of hard treatments, try to remember this distinction: hard treatments tend to offer privacy or light control as their main function. Obviously the valances described in the previous pages don't offer much in the way of privacy or light control, so many people will end up adding a hard treatment along with their valances, the end result being both attractive and functional. Yet, having said that, as hard treatments have become increasingly more stylish and beautiful, some people have opted to hang only hard treatments on their windows and forgo fabric treatments all together.

For now, let me offer you what I call the "food chain" of hard window treatments, starting with the least expensive:

For the sitting room that adjoins a master bedroom, we selected fabrics that coordinated with the bedroom. A triple layer of blinds, shades, and valances fully dress this large window with fabric and texture.

Roller shades

While never described as glamorous, didn't we all start out decking our first apartment in roller shades? They are available in a few different opacity grades, thereby allowing some or no daylight to filter through. You can pay as little as $3 for a roller shade at a national home improvement warehouse. While admittedly roller shades are the bottom rung of the hard treatment ladder, they offer one distinct advantage – they are very easy to customize yourself. You can glue any number of trims to the bottom edge, you can paint the shade itself, or you can glue fabric to the shade; both of the latter options have the added benefit of adding more layers for blocking light.

Mini-blinds

Totally the rage in the eighties, they allowed all college students a touch of class over the roller shades. They still come in a variety of colors, although I usually advise clients to choose either white or off-white to match most window moldings. This allows them the greatest amount of flexibility down the road if/when they want to change the décor in their room. Cost-wise, mini-blinds are on a par with or slightly higher than roller shades. While extremely affordable, the biggest complaint I hear from clients is that they are dust magnets. If you tend to suffer from allergies, unfortunately, they do offer substantial surface space for dust to collect. Rather than dust each vane with that implement that looks like five fuzzy fingers, my solution is to pop the entire blind off the hardware and drop it in the bathtub with some sudsy water. Just a few swishes and the vanes are sparkling clean once again. Shake to dry.

Cellular shades

Otherwise known as honeycomb shades, these shades were developed in the mid-eighties and revolutionized the window shade industry. They are available in hundreds of colors and textures, can be ordered with single, double, or triple honeycomb folds (depending on your need for insulation), and also come in many opacities (depending on your need for light control and privacy).

You can now get cellular shades in a top down-bottom up version, which simply means you can pull one set of cords and the shade rises up from the bottom, or pull a second set of cords, and the shade drops down from the top. This feature is particularly nice over a Jacuzzi, for example, where you would like some sunlight to pour in through your windows, but still require privacy. The top down feature gives you the same light and privacy balance as would a café curtain.

Regional variations across the country not withstanding, cellular shades will cost significantly more than mini-blinds.

Sheer horizontal shades

If you remember the Venetian blinds of the fifties, sheer horizontal shades are a much more sophisticated and stylish interpretation of this horizontal blind. They are made with fabric (not metal) vanes suspended between two sheer fabric facings. The most wonderful aspect of sheer horizontal shades, aside from their physical beauty, is their versatility; they can be fully closed for complete privacy, fully opened to reveal the view outside, or closed, with their vanes tilted parallel to the floor, which offers some privacy while allowing filtered sunlight to stream in. They are also available in a variety of opacities, from sheer for general use to fully light-blocking for those whose schedules require them to sleep during daylight hours. They are a perfect example of the stylish hard window treatments I mentioned earlier; those that provide beauty and functionality without the addition of soft fabric treatments around them. Sheer horizontal shades will be a larger investment than cellular shades but in my opinion, worth every penny.

Banded box pleat valances add a finishing touch when placed above sheer horizontal shades. Note that the fabric band on the valances matches the upholstery on all of the dining room chairs.

Bamboo shades

What goes around comes around! Back and more popular than ever, the bamboo shades of the seventies have made a stylish comeback. Made from grasses and bamboo, as well as slats of wood and various reeds, these shades add an immediate casual and rustic vibe to any interior. When they are opened, some shades are designed to roll up, and others will sit in overlapping folds against your window. Bamboo shades work well in all but the most formal interiors. I've used them in living rooms that express an ethnic or primitive sensibility, as well as a master bedroom with a British Colonial feel. They would work in a beachside "shabby cottage" style as well as an authentic rustic Arts & Crafts interpretation. Simply put, they are fashion-forward and one of the most versatile shades available today.

Bamboo shades are available at many retail outlets but, of course, are only made to fit standard window dimensions. One fact worth mentioning: It's my experience that almost all of the bamboo shades provide translucent, not opaque privacy, so if you're intending to use these in a bedroom, it's wise to custom order them and pay the small charge to have a cotton liner added.

Bamboo shades are very affordable in the retail outlets ($15-$50, depending on the window size) but are in the same price range as cellular shades when custom-ordered.

Vertical blinds

These remain the ideal treatment for any windows that are wider than they are tall, which includes sliding glass doors, French doors, bay windows, or walls of windows. Vertical blinds have come a long way from the blinds of the seventies that reminded most people of dental office décor (apology to all dentists…). They come in fabric, wood, or aluminum, so there's a style for almost any décor. They can also be cut to fit many specialized window sizes such as arches, angles, and bay and corner windows.

Vertical blinds can stand alone as the only treatment you add to a window. They come with their own head rail or "valance" that's designed to cover the sliding mechanism. This head rail lends a neat and tidy look to the blind, should you choose not to add an additional valance. Having said that, many of my clients have opted to have a simple valance made in a fabric that matches the other fabrics in the space, and placed over the vertical head rail. This is a nice touch; the added fabric valance not only pulls the room together by repeating the fabric pattern, but softens the hard edges of the blinds. Vertical blinds are another step up on the window treatment price scale.

Sheer vertical blinds

These hard treatments marry the beauty of sheers with the privacy of vertical blinds and give an overall soft and fluid appearance. Sheer vertical blinds are very similar to standard vertical blinds, except the vanes are softer and are encased in a translucent fabric facing. With a turn of the wand, the vanes will rotate, allowing you to decide on the degree of light control and privacy. They can be fully opened to one side like standard vertical blinds, or can be built to split in the middle, thereby allowing a full view of the outside world. Sheer vertical blinds tend to be more costly than regular vinyl or aluminum vertical blinds, but if you're looking for a chic and elegant step up from the hard look of standard verticals, they are worth the investment.

Wood shutters and wood blinds

This last category of hard window treatments typically represents the largest financial investment. Both horizontal wood blinds and wood shutters can be made from hardwoods such as oak, ash, and cherry, and come in a variety of attractive finishes. While typically the most expensive hard window treatments, both blinds and shutters are also available in wood alternatives, such as composite material and resins, which are the ideal solution if you're on a budget, or if you live in an area where the windows are exposed

For this music room, my client liked the look of layered window treatments. Wooden shutters provide privacy on the lower half of the windows, pleated shades provide privacy for the upper half, and a jaunty stagecoach blind tops it all off.

to high heat, humidity, or other extreme climate conditions. "Faux woods" are much less likely to fade, warp, or crack in these situations.

Wood shutters and horizontal wood blinds can provide a country rustic appeal or an elegant traditional sophistication, depending on the color of their stain. Natural and dark wood stains tend to look the most casual, adding tremendous personality to a Gentlemen's library, a family room with a casual ski lodge style, or a bedroom with a British West Indies tropical style, just to name a few. White painted shutters and blinds, on the other hand, look a bit more formal and are quite at home in a bedroom done in country cottage style, an airy and open Florida-style living room filled with wicker, or a kitchen decorated in the true French Provincial style with boisterous colorful print textiles. Wood blinds and wood shutters are available with a variety of features and benefits, such as decorative tapes for the blinds and tilt features for the shutters. Thoroughly research all of your options before you make a purchase.

While highly versatile, both horizontal wood blinds and wood shutters are heavy-looking treatments. If your room is small, these products may overwhelm the window, and in fact, the entire room. Additionally, some window openings and casings aren't deep enough for the product to be inner-mounted. If they can't be inner-mounted inside your window casings, make sure you like the look of outer-mounted woods. Unequivocally, the most important aspect when considering horizontal wood blinds and wood shutters is to have a professional measure your dimensions and install the finished product. *This is not a do-it-yourself project*.

So you see, there's a tremendous amount of variety in both style and price point when it comes to hard window treatments. Based on your budget, your style décor, and your need for privacy and light control, hopefully you can now decide which option, if any, is for you.

Chapter Eight
Color Wisdom

A Quick Feng Shui Primer On The Power Of Color

If you're now even mildly interested in the concepts of Feng Shui, here's a good place to start. I asked my associate Christine Wojnar, who provides the Feng Shui consultations for my company, to give me a quick reference guide to color according to Feng Shui parameters, and here's what she provided.

"Color is a big subject in Feng Shui. There are five elements and their associated colors that elicit specific energies in your home. They are:

• *Black* or *blue*, associated with water energy, support inner work, helping us to concentrate, contemplate, meditate, and handle creative endeavors. Blue can slow the heart and breathing rates and lower blood pressure. It can be used to increase coolness, to calm, and to create privacy.

• *Green* is associated with wood energy, that of growth, decisiveness, and action. It can motivate internal change.

• *Red* is associated with fire, which supports life energy. It's the color of blood, and can increase heart rate, respiration, and blood pressure. It can also promote activity and alleviate depression. It's clearly the color of passion and love.

• *Yellow* is associated with earth energy, representing Mother Earth. It can cheer, infuse with hope, clarify, and elevate mental activity. It also creates a sense of stability and nurturing. Yellow is often used for children with dyslexia to help improve focus.

• *White* and *metallic colors* are associated with metal energy. They can support carefulness and focus, as well as purity.

Yin and yang are also associated with color. Warmer colors are yang and promote more activity, while the cooler yin colors promote relaxation.

Feng Shui also goes further than the primary colors – mixing these colors can take on characteristics of two or more elements.

Salmon, a combination of yellow/orange and red/orange, holds the qualities of orange, influenced at both ends of the spectrum by red and yellow. This is a unique balance of earth and fire elements that's quite harmonious.

Salmon contains more red pigment than yellow, indicating slightly more fire energy. This represents the heart, fusion to place, and attachment to life. Use salmon to call attention to the heart of a space, create a sense of abundance, and encourage conversation.

Turquoise, being blue/green, evokes the qualities of wood and water. Blue is inward, contemplative, relaxing, and helps with concentration; green is alive, peaceful, fresh, new growth, nurturing. Turquoise augments the aliveness, allowing for movement and growth.

Lavender, a mix of the qualities of blue and purple (which itself is blue and red; its energy is water with some fire), can evoke a sense of calm, spirituality, peace, relaxation, prayer, contemplation, and quiet. You can use lavender to minimize high activity, calm a stressful situation, create a special space, and heighten a sense of spirituality. For these reasons, lavender is better not used in areas where conversation is encouraged or where high activity is necessary."

It could be a fun exercise to go through your home and evaluate what colors dominate your space. Many traditional and/or conservative designers maintain that your entire home should have one cohesive color palette throughout its entirety. I don't agree. I like decorating every room for its intended purpose. As long as the colors flow seamlessly from room to room, who says they have to be in the same palette? But balance is paramount. A room too high in fire energy may produce too much activity, no down time. A room, on the other hand, filled entirely with cold blue tones is exactly that: cold and sometimes uninviting. Start by evaluating your color scheme and proceed with joy and rapture!

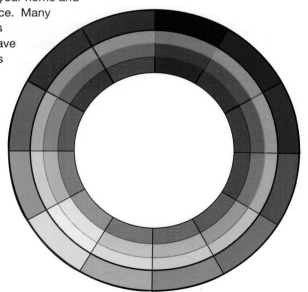

This space is all about rich color. Paint is used very effectively as you move from room to room, colors changing with each turn. What makes it all work is the fact that all of the paint choices are alike in hue concentration.

Instantly Transform A Room With Paint

There's nothing that updates the look and feel of a room for less time, energy, and cash than painting the walls. Moreover, once the job is complete, if it's not what you expected, or what you think you can live with, you can easily paint over it.

Choosing a color

Consider trying colors that sit in the middle of the average paint fan. The top one or two colors tend to be too pastel, and lack the punch found on the third and fourth "steps" of the fan. If you're really feeling bold, paint adjoining rooms in different but compatible colors, such as butternut and nutmeg, or celadon green and soft clay. Or get really bold and paint adjacent walls in the same *room* different colors. Just make sure you end one color and begin the other at a natural line of demarcation, such as where one wall ends and the other begins. When using multiple colors in one room, also try to stay at the same "step" on the color fan; that way you're consistent in the concentration of hue from wall to wall or room to room.

Before you embark on a painting project, it's prudent to take the extra time to test out a few paint colors before you just dive in and paint. Lighting drastically affects the way paint will look in a room, so don't assume the color on the paint chip will look exactly as it will on your walls. I usually have my clients select three paint colors for each room. Some paint companies now make small trial jars of paint, enough to cover a 2x2-foot area. Another company even offers poster-size paint boards with the actual paint used for accuracy – you just tape it to your wall to test the color – no painting necessary. So easy! However, if you can't use one of these trial options, it's still worth ordering a quart of three different paint colors to see which you prefer. (One painter I know uses the rejected paints as his primer coat so they won't necessarily go to waste). Ideally, paint the different colors next to each other, and repeat this process in both the darkest and lightest sections of the room. Look at the paint in broad daylight and in the evening so there will be no surprises. (I once had a friend who painted his study in the evening, in what he thought was soft cantaloupe. By morning, his office was ablaze with glowing orange walls.)

With color this concentrated, you can often dispense with a lot of the accessories. The color is the accessory.

Choosing a finish

Which finish should you select? Most paint companies offer at least five, sometimes seven, finishes of paint, starting with the chalkiest flat to the shiniest gloss, with eggshell, satin, and semi-gloss in between.

In a bathroom, I almost always use gloss or semi-gloss, even on the walls. I just don't want to deal with peeling paint in two years, despite the efforts of the most effective bathroom exhaust fan.

In most other rooms, I like the slight sheen of a satin finish (or, depending on the brand, pearl finish). Both of these finishes leave a lovely patina that's not chalky like flat paint and is infinitely easier to clean. I like to use a semi-gloss or gloss on the trim in these rooms; the shinier finish highlights the trim, and provides a nice contrast with the satin finish on the walls. This finish is also easier to clean, especially important on moldings such as window frames and door trim, which tend to attract fingerprints.

A little tip to the landlords and landladies out there: paint *all* of your rental property with semi-gloss or gloss paint – it cleans up in a snap.

Painting techniques

So now you've selected your new wall color and finish and have viewed it in both daytime and evening light. You may want to consider experimenting with any of the multitude of faux painting techniques, such as ragging, sponging, and marbling, to name just a few.

Or tape off your wall and paint vertical stripes over the existing paint by simply using glaze. If you're really fashion-forward, use one of the hottest new iridescent or metallic glazes. Try painting your walls a soft clay tone and alternate painting stripes with a metallic copper glaze. This is an amazing treatment for an elegant dining room that looks smashing with both wood-toned and painted black furniture.

If you decide you'd love to try a faux treatment, perhaps a mural, but want to leave the application to a professional, make sure they will supply you with sample boards before they paint your walls. Your idea of "Tuscany Hillside at Early Dawn" may be quite different from theirs. Most professionals I've used will always create a few sample boards for the client to approve, before they start applying paint to the walls. And if you decide to paint the base coat on your walls before the painter comes in to do the decorative work, make sure you ask them if they have a preference for what they like to use as a base/primer coat. One muralist I used always wanted her walls to be painted in eggshell finish before she began her artistry. Another preferred that all walls be primed with a special "set coat" done only by her painter to avoid mishaps. So save yourself some time and money by planning ahead.

Adding life to your rooms

If you've lived with white or linen white paint all of your life, adding color is a big step, but a wonderful one at that. You may be a bit shocked initially when the color is up, but breathe deeply and give your eyes a chance to get used to the hue. Sometimes it takes five to seven days before you become acclimated. But remember, the paint looks most intense and concentrated when the room is empty, so as you begin to fill in your furnishings and belongings, the color will be less dominant.

Finally, one great benefit of adding medium- to bold-toned color on your walls is that it makes such a design statement that those with minimal furnishings need not feel compelled to purchase any more. The paint actually becomes an accessory much like lamps and artwork. The rich color carries and fills the room in a way that *no* linen white wall ever could. How's that for gorgeous?!

The painter tried talking my client out of using this shade. After I fired him (just kidding), my client followed my advice and couldn't have been more thrilled with the result. Burnt cantaloupe bathed the walls of this comfortable three-season porch, and created a warm and cozy space.

In this dramatic dining room, claret red crushed velvet draperies were chosen to compliment the claret red paisley design in the wallpaper.

Have Some Red In Your Home, Somewhere

Bringing red into your rooms is an immediate way to infuse them with passion, energy, and excitement. Don't panic. You don't need red in every room, especially if some already have a lot of fire energy to begin with. How do you know if you already have fire energy in your space? According to the principles of Feng Shui, fire energy is present in any color that has red in the mix, which can include orange, rust, purple, and plum. For example, we all know that orange is a mix of red and yellow, yet if the orange is leaning more toward red, the result is fire energy. Conversely, if the orange is a more sunshine yellow-orange, then the energy is translated as earth (yellow) energy, not fire energy. Another example: purple is a mix of red and blue, yet if the shade leans more towards blue (violet), the energy becomes water energy. Conversely, purples that have more red in the mix, such as plum and grape, will bring more fire energy to the space.

So you don't need to worry about rooms that already have enough fire energy in them. I'm thinking more about the perpetually neutral rooms that need to come alive with a jolt of red. Or the fully pastel rooms that will wake up when you add one or two watermelon- or geranium-colored pillows. Hmmm, you're starting to like this idea, but are wondering, "Which shade of red should I choose?" Image consultants will tell you that everyone can wear the color red – you just need to find the correct shade. It's the same for interiors.

You must first ask yourself: is my room predominantly dressed in warm or cool tones? Then try to expand your impression of the word red. Warm reds are close to orange on the color wheel, and include all these luscious shades: vermilion orange, tomato, brick and mandarin red, and Valentine red. Cool reds are closer to purple on the color wheel, and include burgundy, claret, scarlet, and George Washington red.

Even the most earth-toned room replete with greens, tans, and browns will look awakened with a splash of red. Consider adding toss pillows, a chenille throw, and pillar candles in a warm brick red or cinnabar. If your room's palette tends to be cool and is currently adorned in light to medium blues, infuse it with the passion of red, but choose cooler versions such as watermelon or geranium red (these are pinky reds that prevent the room from looking patriotic!). Deep navy and teal, on the other hand, require deep brick red, burgundy, or a bluer red to balance their intensity, but nonetheless add pizzazz.

And if you're up for a real adventure, consider doing a room in one of the following color combinations, all of which use a fabulous red in a very fashion-forward interpretation:

- fuchsia & pumpkin
- claret & tangerine
- brick red & chocolate brown
- claret & plum
- pastel pink & cocoa brown

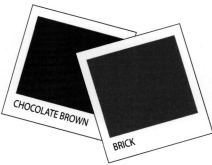

CHOCOLATE BROWN

BRICK

So you see, there are almost countless ways to inject the passion and excitement of red into any interior. But I caution you; The results may be downright intoxicating. What a wonderful problem to encounter…

Using red in your home doesn't have to mean using the boldness of valentine red. These clients preferred the
subtle richness of a brick red in their living room, so this understated scroll-patterned wallpaper fit the bill.

In this extraordinary mantel display, the walls are richly hued but all other accessories are neutral. It's the sensuous curves of the vessels along with the "floating spheres" that make this design element spectacular.

Add Texture To Un-Neutralize Neutrals!

While bold and beautiful color is enjoying great popularity these days, there's always a large audience in favor of neutrals for their design décor. Neutrals are undeniably soothing, serene, and sophisticated. In a dizzying world of over-stimulation, neutrals are often the shelter from the storm. They're also a common destination for the novice who has set out on his or her first interior decorating journey. Yet, to avoid looking bland, flat, or otherwise uninteresting, neutrals require a design imperative for their survival: texture. Texture can be found in a myriad of places and expressed in a plethora of accessories.

Adding texture on your floors

If you're a fan of hardwood floors, try to select a wood grain that boasts a lot of gorgeous grain, such as oak or maple. The variations in the wood's natural color will add a lot of personality to a neutral room, while providing a stunning foundation to the room's furnishings. If you tend to be a wall-

118

What do shiny fabrics, rattan seating, and a hardwood chest with bamboo panels all have in common? Texture, texture, texture! Use it liberally in your most neutral interiors.

to-wall carpeting enthusiast, a neutral room is the perfect place to try out sculptured or textured carpets. If you're really a trendsetter, go unabashedly into the future with the new shag carpeting or area rugs. The shag of the twenty-first century is made from several straight and curly fibers that have a variety of thicknesses for extreme texture and dimension. Leather shag area rugs, a variation of this theme, will add instant panache to any neutral room.

Adding texture on your walls

The walls, as the backdrop of a room, are particularly important in a neutral décor theme. If you must paint them off-white, consider using one of the many faux techniques such as ragging, combing, or sponging. Using just a bit of any darker hue, faux techniques bring walls from flat to fabulous, while still keeping very much in a neutral palette. Wallpaper lovers will revel in the effect created by grass cloth and faux suede papers.

Adding texture with your accessories

Finally, accessories should include, but aren't nearly limited to, any of the
following textural pieces: woven shades; curtains and pillows in raw silk;
linen, brocades, and embroideries; curly willow sticks in pottery vases;
natural elements such as seashells and tumbled stones; three-dimensional
artwork for the walls, such as masks, tapestries, and wall hangings; and
lastly, mirrors and frames in carved wood, wrought iron, or inlaid shells. Are
you getting the picture? Any accessory that's not flat to the touch will bring
out the best in the most neutral of rooms.

When you add elements to your too-neutral rooms that incorporate texture
that you can either see or feel (or, ideally, both!), you'll inject these spaces with
some badly-needed life and energy. And couldn't we all use more energy?

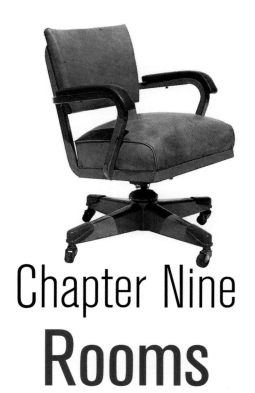

Chapter Nine
Rooms

Make Your Bedroom Your Sanctuary

Is your bedroom an inviting oasis full of soft textures, inspiring colors, and artwork that's meaningful to you? I can just hear all of the mothers of small children out there saying, "Are you crazy?" Kids or no kids, why can't your bedroom be a sanctuary? Are you planning to wait until they leave for college for this project? Did you know that your bedroom is the most important room in your home? Yes, I know the kitchen is considered the heart of the home, but if you're romantically involved, the bedroom trumps even the kitchen… In fact, even if you're happily single and solo, your bedroom is your cocoon, your shelter from the proverbial storm. It needs to be your safe haven for sleeping, intimacy, and recharging your body and soul.

"Sprightly" probably best describes this whimsical bedroom. Even with very little furniture in a space, a few catchy design elements speak volumes. Here we have an interesting combination of starfish floating over a contemporary patchwork quilt. This almost sounds like an oxymoron, but it's in this unexpected union where the interest lies.

What is the *most* important thing you can do to your bedroom right now? Declutter it. Books and magazines are okay, but in the language of Feng Shui, too many stirs up too much energy. Containerize them neatly in a basket or small shelf and edit regularly. Puh-lease tackle the bottles and jars and receipts and keys and coins that are regularly heaped on your bureaus. And the laundry piles? I once had a client tell me that the five-foot pile of laundry on her floor was okay because it was clean. Um… Put it all away please.

How attractive is your bedding? It doesn't have to be an expensive couture design; it can be a beautiful ethnic throw or a horse blanket you brought back from Aspen. But if it's stained, full of moth holes, or – worse, was a gift from an ex-lover who exited your life on unhappy terms – egad! It's time to replace it. Aim for bedding that's soft, ideally coordinates in some way to your window treatments and pillows and *feels* good against your skin (wool itches, right?). And that oh-so-chic rattan – yes rattan – throw pillow I saw recently on someone's bed – no way. Would you put your face on that? Additionally, if your wall-to-wall carpet is stained, purchase inexpensive area rugs and runners (see Area Rugs and Carpeting, page 62). They will instantly enliven the décor.

With these soft hues of butter cream, celadon, and lavender, my client said she felt as if she was sleeping in a box of fondant candy... And that was a good thing!

Now for the artwork: this is really powerful. After a Feng Shui consultation in my own house, I realized that the monkey prints I bought to express my tropical bedroom were, um, scary and evil-looking. I never really loved them, but I thought they would "work" in the space so I bought them. And the large antique map I also bought to express the tropical theme was an image of South Africa, which for me, upon reflection, conjured up images of Apartheid. The point: We all need to pay close attention to what our artwork is really saying to us, especially in our bedrooms. And at the risk of being unpopular, bedrooms are *not* the best place for family photos. A very good friend of ours has a picture of his mother at age five hanging near his bed... Can you say cramped style? Think romance, romance, romance, and if you're currently unattached, display wonderful, smiling, gorgeous pictures of *you*!

Here are the replacement prints we bought for our bedroom, when we figured out that hanging scary-looking monkeys was awful Feng Shui. The prints we chose instead still express the tropical theme I love, and are much more pleasant images. Note how we hung the pictures so the two lions were walking toward, not away from, each other. This small example of symbolism does not go unnoticed in the eyes of Feng Shui.

Finally, make sure you have a decent reading light by your bed. Installing recessed lights over the bed, with a switch by your night table, is a divine luxury everyone should consider. And a few sturdy pillar candles that waft one of your favorite scents are a must.

Now *this* sounds like a cocoon for some serious nesting. You know you want this. Can you really wait until the kids are eighteen to get it?

Happy Kitchens, Happy Owners

Despite your game room, family room, and bar downstairs, where do friends always converge when you entertain? The kitchen. It must be some primal instinct; something from our collective unconscious that keeps bringing us back. Back to wonderful smells and sounds and of course, memories of Mom turning the wild boar on the open pit... I guess my memories are more primitive than most people's.

At least seventy-five percent of all of my clients who have lived in a home they did not build from scratch themselves have been unhappy with their kitchens. Yet it is without a doubt the most daunting renovation to envision and oversee. There are hundreds of good books specifically on renovating and updating kitchens, so ideas are out there and plentiful. Consistent with the spirit of this book, I want to help you muddle through the planning process of redoing a kitchen – not whether you should pick laminate or cherry cabinets, but how do you start to get your arms around the process?

Low-impact kitchen makeovers

But before I do, for those of you who are more interested in ideas on a "low-impact, non-extreme renovation" (see Starting Small, page 44), rest assured that there are many things you can do to update your kitchen without committing yourself to spending a lot of time and money on the project.

If you're tired of your kitchen and don't have the budget or energy for a big renovation, consider these small upgrades: changing the hardware (knobs and pulls) on your cabinetry and replace your light fixture/fan. Pick out the same finish for all of these items; some popular finishes are antiqued bronze (looks like rust), black wrought iron, or brushed silver (looks like pewter). If you have stools or chairs in your kitchen, consider upgrading these while you're at it in the same metal finish. If your barstools are made of wood, changing the seating pads will instantly freshen the overall look. You may be so excited at the change that you may be inspired to keep going with new artwork, curtains, and paint. Good for you!

High-impact kitchen renovations

For the rest of you who know a high-impact renovation is in your future (and haven't been swayed to stick with a low-impact renovation), read on.

Ideally, you've been collecting tear sheets from magazines and have begun to amass a little scrapbook of your own for ideas and inspiration. The more

When interviewing your kitchen
contractor, make sure she or he
will respect your design wishes.
If that means you want them to
design a kitchen around electric
blue cabinets, so be it!

visuals you can give a professional, the better they will serve you. But if you
haven't, it's a good idea to start doing so.

The most common questions I'm asked are, "Who do I hire first? Do I
need an architect? Can a carpenter redo my kitchen?" Many General
Contractors (GCs) are actually what they call design/build firms. If you've
chosen this type of firm, you don't need to hire a separate architect. This
type of GC will not only design your structure, but will also outsource the
structural design and land surveying tasks. If you're renovating your existing
kitchen (or bath) versus adding square footage to your house by way of an
addition, land surveying isn't necessary. Confirm this with your contractor.

Personal bias notwithstanding, bringing in an interior designer during a
renovation is invaluable. GCs honestly don't want to be bothered helping
their clients decide whether they should choose Giallo Santa Cecelia or Uba
Tuba for their granite countertops, and they shouldn't. A good designer
will help you make these choices and help keep the GC and his or her subs
on schedule – this is a win-win situation. You can also *start* with an interior
designer. Many have established relationships with Architects and GCs, so
they act as the point person, or Project Manager, and help bring in all the
other personnel you'll need to get your job done.

Many GCs offer kitchen (and bath) renovation as a specialty. If you decide
to go this route, make sure you're clear on the process. Do they offer both
custom and readily-stocked lines of cabinetry? Is there a showroom where
they'll send you to pick out cabinets and case goods, as well as faucets,

There are countless styles of kitchens to be created, with a plethora of materials from which to choose. I urge you to start a scrapbook of clippings so your contractor can best serve you.

sinks, showers, toilets, light fixtures, and flooring? Or can you decide to buy these items on your own at a home improvement store? Make sure your expectations and those of the GC are the same.

The other way to orchestrate a kitchen (or bath) renovation is to go to a firm that specializes in such. Many have retail storefronts with elaborate showrooms of "sample" kitchens and baths. They almost always create the design plan. You need to ask if they require you to use their installer or if you can use your own carpenter/contractors, assuming you've already chosen them. Most will expect you to buy their cabinetry. Others may sell you just their plans. Inquire as to how you go about getting the other fixtures, such as faucets, lights, flooring etc. Always inquire about lead-time on merchandise and anticipated project completion dates.

Final notes on General Contractors/Kitchen Renovations:

1. Make sure the GC is licensed.

2. Make sure the GC is registered in your state through the Home Improvement Contracting (HIC) Law.

3. Make sure the GC carries adequate liability insurance and workman's compensation insurance.

4. Ask for his or her references, and when you call the references, inquire as to whether their renovation was close in scope (complexity and technical sophistication) to the job you're considering having done.

5. It's prudent to do due diligence on *any* professional. Therefore, consider researching any possible legal allegations by doing a search on the Better Business Bureau website and/or a search engine.

6. Each state has requirements on deposits and payments. Many states stipulate that a contractor cannot ask for more than one-third payment down as a deposit. Confirm your state's regulations.

7. Consider obtaining three bids.

8. Get a written contract and read the fine print.

9. At the beginning of your relationship, ask this general question of your GC, "What will my responsibilities be? What are yours?"

We have all heard of the endless horror stories people experience with renovations. You don't have to be part of those statistics. If you take the time to interview several contractors and contact their references to ensure their legitimacy, you're already on your way to a successful renovation. If you then communicate with your spouse and your contractor throughout the process and *never* assume anything, you're highly likely to have a favorable and maybe even pleasurable overall renovation experience. Good luck!

In the photo on the facing page, the kitchen cabinets are installed right up to the ceiling line. In this photo, the clients requested that space be left open above the cabinets so they could decorate with their favorite possessions. Make sure you specify to your contractor which look you prefer.

Bathrooms Require Extra Ingenuity

Unless you're lucky enough to have an exquisitely large bathroom with space for a chaise lounge and a chair or two, it's intrinsically trickier to get great style translated in bathrooms. Obviously, living rooms, dens, and bedrooms afford all sorts of possibilities with gorgeous textiles. Even dining rooms can be furnished with upholstered chairs, or at least seat cushions, not to mention adequate windows to dress. Bathrooms, on the other hand, require every decorative element to really count, to make a strong statement unto itself.

The easiest way to make a bold statement in a bathroom (and in any other room for that matter) is with the use of rich colors on the walls. I was recently in a small powder room of a client that housed nothing other than a toilet and a small vanity. Luckily, the ceilings were fairly high and a window provided a generous amount of light. And the vanity was anything but pedestrian. The builder was clever enough to supply the room with a white porcelain sink housed in a dark-stained Asian-inspired cabinet and a very stylish and unusual waterfall type faucet. My client's instincts about finishing the room were correct. She asked what I thought of painting the walls a medium-toned olive green. I immediately envisioned capitalizing on the Eastern theme by adding a few dark stained accessories such as a wicker tissue box, wicker wastebasket, and shelf above the toilet. For the window, because privacy was already provided by a pleated shade, we did an unusual treatment of tacking bamboo sticks and faux palm fronds across the top of the window. This diminutive room was small in size but high on style predominantly because of the power of paint.

I'm also asked regularly about hanging wallpaper and artwork in bathrooms. I almost always recommend against wallpaper, because of the obvious issue of moisture. Artwork, however, is another story. Clearly, I wouldn't hang an expensive or personally valuable piece of artwork in a bathroom, even one that has adequate ventilation. But that hardly means your accessory options are limited. Over the years, in bathrooms I've hung painted tiles, flat-sided vases with curly willow sticks, tribal masks, framed posters and prints, and silk flower wreaths, just to name a few. In a little boy's western bathroom (see Innovative Accessorizing, page 76), we hung a collection of cowboy hats on one wall and a real life lasso on the other! Wicker and wrought iron shelves are not only lovely, but functional for storage. The addition of sconces will not only add extra illumination but will offer more character than will most standard overhead light fixtures.

Obviously, if you're in the position to custom-build your bathroom and can pick stunning tiles, wonderful! However, many of us just want to create the most stylish bathroom we can, given what came with the house. And you can create a big "WOW" factor if you're willing to go bolder on the paint, and be creative with your accessories.

In this perky bathroom, to soften the unavoidable hard porcelain surfaces, we repeated the use of playful fabric in three places: the valance, the shower curtain, and the toilet seat cover.

One final note: If you're building a bathroom from scratch, don't be seduced into buying colorful fixtures (i.e., tub, toilet, and sink). You'll likely tire of their color over time and feel stuck with the limited design options they provide. While I'm the original color enthusiast in all other areas, in this case, white and almond porcelain fixtures are the wisest choice.

And speaking of building a bath from scratch, don't feel compelled to place tile on ninety-five percent of the wall and floor surfaces; your bath will start to resemble a health club. Painted walls are just fine in a bath, but consider using a semi-gloss or gloss paint finish that will stand up to the moisture.

All the hard porcelain and ceramic surfaces notwithstanding, it's entirely possible to create an attractive and inviting oasis, even in the smallest of bathrooms. And it's worth putting some effort into creating this yourself. When you roll out of bed every morning, what kind of room do you want greeting you and welcoming you to the new day?

Who said bathrooms have to be pedestrian? Uncommon and artsy best describe the sensibility of these bathrooms. In a typically small space as a bathroom, make sure all of your design elements really count.

In this guest bath, we chose to add decorative elements not unlike those found in a living room or bedroom, such as lush fabrics and upscale furnishings and light fixtures. Note the three pictures hanging above the console: they were once part of a 1992 calendar that featured sepia-toned turn-of-the-century Olympians. Style is where you find it.

Home Offices Can Be More Than Utilitarian

With the explosion of home-based businesses and tele-commuting, I'm often asked to provide decorating ideas for home offices. My goal is always to maximize productivity and efficiency without sacrificing aesthetics.

Since there are already many good books on creating the perfect home office, I thought I would offer a slightly fresh perspective on the subject that involves one of my favorite topics: Feng Shui.

Also, don't forget to make your other work environments more comfortable and efficient as well, by applying the following suggestions to your cubicle or office out of the home.

Succeed with your power corner

Locate and embellish your power corner. This is one of the most significant efforts you can make to increase prosperity. According to Feng Shui principles, every room has a power corner, the corner that's at a direct diagonal to its entrance. If your power corner is cluttered with files, boxes,

Notice the embellished "power corner" of my office: it's functional and beautiful at the same time.

and general disorganization, your business is already suffering. My power corner in my own office needed a makeover several years ago. The recommendations from my Feng Shui consultant were easy and almost immediately I saw an increase in both sales and my own productivity.

We made three changes: (1) We hung certificates of achievement and framed pictures of interiors I had done on the two adjacent walls of my power corner. (2) Additionally, what was once a cluttered credenza of office files and equipment became a stylish surface. We placed the copier on one end, a printer on the other end, and in the middle, we placed a striking lamp, a small plant, and a beautiful scented candle. This changed what was once a very crowded utilitarian space into a functional and aesthetically-pleasing space. Resource files were organized and placed in bins under the fabric-covered credenza. (3) Because the only possible placement of my desk left my back facing the door when I worked at my computer, we hung a large carved mirror on the wall in front of me, so I could see anyone walking in the door behind me.

Be careful about used furniture

Be prudent when furnishing your office with antiques. While I love previously-owned furniture for its quality, beauty, character, and (sometimes) affordability, the principles of Feng Shui caution against the use of using furniture if you don't know its history. You don't know if bankruptcy or a similar misfortune beset the original owners that could then bring negative energy into your space – not something you want in a room connected to your financial prosperity! If you can't live without the rich look of the past, at least consider having a space clearing done when the furniture enters the office. This will clear any potential negative energy from the piece, thereby allowing a fresh new start for pieces new to you.

Prioritize your files

According to Feng Shui, giving your important papers and files the respect they deserve will encourage prosperity for your business. Keep them off the floor, and ideally not under a desk or table – you don't want the backbone of your finances sitting among dust bunnies and crumbs, do you? Higher shelves and bookcases are better for client files, as well as financial files such as stock certificates, investment documents, and property deeds. Additionally, leave adequate physical space between client files. A drawer that's stuffed to capacity doesn't leave much room for new business, does it?

Inspire yourself

Bring into your office that which inspires you and brings you joy, as long as it doesn't drive you to distraction. As I mentioned earlier, my office is filled with watercolor paintings I did as a five-year-old, and the walls are bathed in yummy hues of orange and raspberry sherbet. Everything about my office says creativity, which keeps me stimulated and always thinking outside of the box. What will bring life into your home office?

Installations for better function

Aside from the fascinating perspective Feng Shui brings to the home office, keep in mind that many home offices are located in spare bedrooms, which present their own unique challenges, lack of lighting and adequate storage especially. While you're doing your home office makeover, make absolutely sure you have enough lighting, both ambient and task lighting, and have equipped the one possible closet in the space to accommodate business needs, not hangers full of clothes. Installing white wire shelving systems and wicker bins are the least

When we unearthed the watercolor paintings I did as a five-year-old, there was no doubt in my mind where they should be displayed. This office is all about encouraging creativity.

expensive and most attractive ways to bring order and beauty to a standard bedroom closet. So why not experiment? Try a few of these simple but powerful adjustments. Change is good. Watch your prosperity rise.

Originally just a small sitting room off a living room, the addition of the custom-made built-in defines this space as the perfect home office. The faux linen effect on the walls keeps the room soft and neutral, allowing the accessories and artifacts (and extensive frog collection!) in the built-in to really shine.

Create A Sacred Space Somewhere In Your Home

Whether you can devote a whole room to this purpose or just a corner of a room, the adults in the home have a right to a quiet space of their own. I won't tell you how many ten-room homes I've been in that dedicate the majority of the rooms to the children. Is this really necessary? What happened to kids playing outside in fresh air, be it snow or sunshine? Parents out there: reclaim some space of your own! Ideally, have a room of your own for reading, meditating, watching the occasional favorite TV show, or writing in your journal.

I laugh when I remember visiting my college roommate MaryAnn, who designed a special feature in her long double parlor. One end was for their three active sons, and the other end was for her and her husband Ken. The boys knew where the line was drawn and that they were not to cross it and spill their books, toys, and clutter into Mommy and Daddy's space. This may sound extreme, but it was designed in good humor and love. Also, when Mommy and Daddy were in their space, whether they were relaxing or reading, the boys were to give their parents the downtime they needed.

The boys knew to play among themselves at these times. The boys, in general, were raised to understand and respect boundaries and were taught that the world doesn't revolve around them, nor do they "own" the entire house. How novel.

In your own home, if you can't devote an entire room to such guilty pleasures, certainly you can carve out a corner of the den or family room. Allow yourself a cozy chair with an ottoman, a light for reading, and a side surface to hold your teacup or wine glass, not to mention a burning votive candle. If your life is missing downtime (whose isn't?), embellish this area with additional examples of tranquility and relaxation, such as special artwork, statues, shells, or stones from nature. Most important, surround yourself with symbols that reflect your dreams. They could be photos of a tranquil beach scene from the Caribbean, or perhaps a red glass heart that symbolizes the romantic love you want to draw into your life. You don't have to be a practicing Buddhist to know that we are all more likely to attract into our lives the objects of our focus; that which we not only think about, but physically display in our environments.

What we think about, we tend to talk about. And what we talk about tends to manifest itself in our lives. As Life Coach Cheryl Richardson says, if you take care of yourself first by practicing extreme self-care, then you'll have more to give to your family and friends. Are you sure you're attracting the right things into your life?

In this sweet little meditation room, where the client goes to decompress, we chose a serene robin's egg blue color for the walls and filled the space with calming accessories such as candles, tumbled river rocks, a water fountain, and prints of Chinese calligraphy.

A comfy spot to lay your head, a side table for your tea (or vino), and a decent reading light: the perfect spot to open the mail and unwind after a long day.

Chapter Ten
Spatial Elements

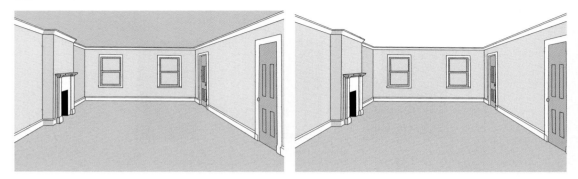

Notice the dramatic difference achieved by painting your ceiling a darker hue than the walls. This is the perfect antidote to a cavernous room with very high ceilings.

Create Illusions With Your Ceilings

Part of the fun of my job is to create solutions for some of the challenges that typical houses present. The most common structural challenge is too-high ceilings. Luckily, this problem area has easy solutions. You can balance this issue by creating illusions with color and lighting.

If your ceilings are very high, almost too cavernous, consider painting them a darker color than your walls. Try cappuccino tan on the walls and mocha brown on the ceilings; or soft celadon on the walls, and sage green on the ceilings. Very fashion-forward!

I once worked with a client who lived in a gorgeous Victorian home that was graced with ten-foot ceilings. Along with the built-in china closets and lovely wood molding, this house offered a great opportunity to minimize its cavernous feeling. There was picture molding attached to all of the walls, yet it was attached about sixteen inches down from the ceiling line. So along with painting the ceilings a darker hue than the walls, we brought the darker hue down to just above the picture molding. The rich color enveloped the whole room and created a cozy canopy of warmth.

There are additional ways to offset a ceiling that is too high. One way is to bring your fixtures down by replacing surface-mounted light fixtures with elegant hanging fixtures. Chandeliers are now available in a myriad of retro and contemporary styles, so don't assume all chandeliers have tons of faceted crystals. Another clever trick is to shine a spot light at the base of a tall tree (real or faux), such as a Ficus. The shadow created will grow beyond the tree itself, thereby adding a taller element in the space. In the interest of good Feng Shui, I do urge you, however, *not* to install dark beams overhead. They are ominous and bring a sense of danger to space, despite what popular designers tell you. So try to play around with the elements in your room – you might just be able to address a problem while creating unexpected style and drama in your space!

Create Illusions With Your Windows

In addition to creating illusions with your ceilings, there are a few more visual tricks you need to know to play with windows in order to create the visual effect you want in your spaces.

One of the most common errors I see in decorating windows is when clients overdress very small windows, adding multiple layers of swags, jabots, and sometimes sheers. In a window that may measure only thirty-six inches wide, this is far too heavy a treatment. Furthermore, clients will hang these layers directly on the window moldings, leaving about twelve inches of actual window uncovered.

Instead of cluttering up your windows with unnecessary fabric, mount the curtain rods above the molding, close to the ceiling, and beyond the molding to the left and right of the window. Provided there's enough wall space and no interference with artwork or built-ins, mounting rods beyond the window allows the majority of the window, and therefore light, to show, while giving the illusion of a grander, more stately window.

As you can see in the picture to the right, this Colonial home had a beautiful corner built-in china cabinet, which made hanging window treatments in this small dining room quite tricky. So we decided to treat the two adjacent walls and the built-in as one window, if you will. By mounting the window treatments not only above the windows, but ten inches beyond each window, we were able to hang the lavish silk swags and jabots the client requested. The most important choice on this installation was the decision to hang only one panel per window. The overall effect is striking: upon entering the room, one immediately notices the center china cabinet built-in and sees

By mounting the valance right up to the ceiling line, we give the illusion of taller windows and reduce the amount of light lost by the window treatment.

Hanging drapery panels on both sides of both windows would have accentuated the smallness of the windows in this elegant dining room. Don't be afraid to get creative when spaces throw you a design challenge.

the layers of elegant silk fabric surrounding it. Maximum light is retained because we left a full thirty inches of exposed window; this client chose to diffuse the light and add privacy with cellular shades.

The result was a strikingly elegant window treatment: privacy when needed, optimal light retention, and the added illusion of taller windows and higher ceilings.

Had I been the designer in this home, I would have suggested we paint out the radiators to match the walls. They stand out just a bit too much for my liking.

Hiding Ugly Ducklings In Your Home

Doesn't every home you've ever lived in have the occasional eyesore? You know; odd water pipes overhead in the kitchen of an 1800s Mansard colonial house. Or perhaps big puffy air ducts running along the ceiling of your chic and pricey downtown loft. How about really unsightly radiators plopped down right where you'd like to put a piece of furniture? Some of these elements would cost too much to remove or relocate, so we designers are always thinking of clever ways to disguise them, or at the very least, help them blend in a bit more. While an entire book could be written on this subject, I'll offer up solutions to the most common complaints I've heard from my clients.

The easiest way to not notice some of the aforementioned eyesores is to paint them the same color as the background they are up against. Just be sure to use the correct paint; in the case of water pipes or radiators, you must use heat resistant paint or at least prime them in heat resistant primer before you paint them.

Feel stuck with an outdated backsplash in your kitchen? Did you know there is now primer available for painting tile as well? The success of the tile backsplash project is all in the proper preparation of the tiles, but this *is* a do-it yourself project. First and foremost, the tiles must be in good condition. If grout needs to be scraped and replaced, allow forty-eight hours for the new grout to cure before you proceed with the painting. Once the new grout has dried, you must sand the tiles with very fine aluminum oxide sandpaper. This will remove all of the gloss on the tile without scratching it. Wipe down all of the dust and dry with a cloth. Apply two coats of high adhesion interior latex binding primer, allowing each coat to dry thoroughly before the next step. Once the primer has completely dried, you can paint over the tiles with an acrylic latex semi-gloss or gloss in your choice of colors. Voila! The seventies blades of wheat are forever gone from your backsplash! Please keep in mind, however, that this project is only designed for tile that is *not* directly exposed to water. If you have a tub or shower enclosure that also bugs you, I recommend calling a resurfacing professional for this project.

Speaking of strange kitchen occurrences, I recently worked in the kitchen of the 1800s Mansard colonial I mentioned earlier. Originally, I assume, there was attractive wainscoting along the kitchen walls. After several renovations and additions of wallboard to hide who knows what, the current owners, my lovely clients, were left with walls that actually overhung the wainscoting. This was kind of dreadful, but they weren't up for gutting the walls and replacing wallboards. Instead, I implored my trusty painter Mike and his brother Will to do the best they could with spackle, and they obliged. We then opted not to paint the wainscoting one color and the walls another color, which typically is an attractive thing to do. In this case, we didn't want to highlight the obvious imperfections of the walls. By painting the entire wall, ceiling to floor, one color, we downplayed what was left of the kooky wainscoting. Of course, the addition of gorgeous window treatments and accessories further drew your eye away from the wall. Ah, another eyesore minimized by the use of paint!

Another common complaint I hear is what to do with the seemingly thousands of cords that accompany audio and computer components. If going wireless isn't your style, you can use what's called a cable management kit. This is essentially a long tube of bendable plastic that encloses your collection of cords in one tight tube that neatly

A fully-enclosed home office was the perfect solution for this family. No unsightly wires, no piles of paper; simply close the doors when company is coming and it looks like just another handsome piece of furniture.

hangs down behind your components. If you have several cords that are currently running along your floor or baseboard (i.e., cable wires, extension cords, etc.), you can hide them with a cord cover kit. Simply slip the wires into the rigid PVC channel, peel off the adhesive backing, and place the channel along any flat surface. This looks particularly tidy when affixed on the bottom of a wall, just above your cove molding. You can even paint the channel to blend in with your décor, further hiding these eyesores. Most kits come with thirty-six inches of channel, and all of the caps and couplings necessary to turn a corner on your walls. This is a good alternative to adding electrical outlets, especially in an exterior wall of an old home, where "fishing" power wires may be very dicey.

What to do if you have unsightly exercise equipment or a small home office tucked away in a corner of a room that you would like to be hidden? The easiest solution would be to purchase a decorative three- or four-panel screen. They are available in a myriad of décor styles, such as bamboo, louvered panels, or painted scenes. You can also make one yourself with fabric panels pulled tightly across wood frames. A real luxury would be to add little wheels on the bottom of the screen panels to avoid back strain when you move the screen. In the case of the small home office, there are literally hundreds of armoires available that will house your computer components, as well as provide shelf and drawer storage, and will hide everything away behind closed doors when the day's work is done. For the bargain conscious, you can purchase an armoire made of MDF (medium density fiberboard) or a similar laminate for a few hundred dollars. Armoires made of an attractive hardwood such as oak, cherry, or walnut will run anywhere between $500 to $2,000 or more, depending on the source.

With so many clever options available, there simply is no longer any excuse to live with ugly ducklings in your home. Go ahead; identify one that has been nagging you for some time and make a plan to fix it. Once it's completed, I know you'll thank me for it. You're very welcome.

Don't Weigh Yourself Down

I've seen many rooms that were otherwise pulled together very nicely, with the décor theme nicely expressed throughout, yet next to two fluffy overstuffed chairs sat a scrawny glass and iron-legged table that looked as if it would collapse if someone sneezed nearby. Or in a country dining room where the focal piece was a rough-hewn substantial maple table, I saw four delicate French Provincial chairs. In this case, not only were the chairs stylistically incompatible, but they didn't carry enough heft to balance the table, and ideally, there should have been six, not four chairs.

This isn't to say that eclectic decorating isn't fabulous. Mixing styles and genres is all the rage today, but some rooms push beyond the word eclectic and start to look simply mismatched. I admit, this is sometimes a hard call to make. If you find yourself decorating a room in, for example,

This bright and cheery kitchen achieves balance because all of the objects have similar visual weight. The bold French Provincial wallpaper looks positively yummy next to the simple lines of the oak table and chairs.

The beauty of this sun-drenched space lies in its balance. While the wallpaper is a busy floral and the chandelier and chairs are distinctly ornate, the room isn't fussy. A solid wooden table would have added unwanted weightiness, yet the columns provide the needed heft for this otherwise ethereal space.

a rough-hewn country style and you're afraid there's already too much heaviness present, you'll need to add "relief" in other ways. Rather than placing a skimpy glass table between those two overstuffed chairs, choose a round wood chest, or a marble tabletop on a curved wrought iron base. Or better yet, a wicker or a wood table, painted in the colors that match the fabrics in the room. You'll be adding the correct heft without making the pieces look too boxy or clunky.

Too little visual weight is a reverse, but just as common, problem – this is when a room doesn't have a focal point, or when all of the pieces and accessories lack definition. Designers will often say this type of room isn't "grounded" or is too "airy," where the pieces seem to float in the space – and not in a good way! The rooms almost seem to cry out for an anchor.

I've seen this dilemma in a few situations, including a room done entirely in pastels. Pastels are lovely, but unless you like the idea of living in an Easter egg, you'll want to select some ways of grounding the room. The simplest way to achieve this end is with an area rug (placed over hard wood or directly on neutral broadloom carpet). Try to resist buying a pastel rug; instead, consider deeper versions of the colors already in the room, such as celadon green, cappuccino tan, Nantucket blue, geranium pink, or smoky plum. These tones will rescue the room from looking too childlike, yet maintain the integrity of the pastel style.

On a final note, now that mid-century modern style has resurfaced with wild popularity, take care to give these rooms enough heft and definition as well. A room full of chrome and low straight-lined furniture can run the risk of looking overly industrial and cold. Bring some sexy curves to this room with luscious blown glass vases and lamps with fifties-inspired sculptural bases and squat shades. Top it off with a fabulous long tufted leather ottoman (in cherry red if you can stand it) proudly perched on a leather shag area rug! Too fab for words.

Give Your Eyes A Break – Utilize Negative Space

Especially you folks who adore traditional décor, replete with chintz fabrics and porcelain plates, it's important to resist the temptation to fill every corner of your rooms with objects. Humans need visual relief from stimulation, and this is what negative space provides. Somewhere in my travels, I once read an article recommending that all four corners of a room should be free of objects so as not to over-clutter the room. I don't think it's necessary to keep *all* four corners empty, but I think it's prudent to aim for not filling *every* corner. To be sure, a room can look very stylish and attractive with an occasional Ficus tree or pole lamp in one or two of the room's corners.

The same principle applies to hanging artwork. Not every small space on a wall needs to be filled. A good technique is to hang what you consider to be the most important or your favorite pieces first, then survey the room. Does it still need more art, does it look bare – or do those few empty walls, in fact, look like an intentional and judicious use of negative space that keeps the focus on the important pieces?

How about your counters and table surfaces? On page 16, I discussed the importance of decluttering your home before you even entertain the possibility of redecorating. Along those lines, look at those places in

This busy couple juggles high-powered careers and family everyday. They needed a bedroom that was nothing less than serene. Soft olive hues for the walls and minimal accessories make this urban country space their shelter from the proverbial storm.

your home where objects seemingly reproduce overnight while you sleep. Kitchen counters, kitchen islands/peninsulas, dining room tables and buffets, bookcases, and hallway entrance tables; all of these surfaces tend to perpetually collect clutter so that you can't even identify your design theme anymore. Once you've gotten into the habit of living by the C.A.R.D. principle, why not play some "tough love" with the excess decorative accessories that have accumulated?

Look at every trinket and vase and statuette and box that resides on these surfaces and ask yourself: do I love it? As I stated before, if it isn't an "absolute *yes*," it's time to donate it to someone who just may fall in love with it at first sight.

Call it negative space; call it breathing room; call it making way for more grace to enter your life (another Cheryl Richardson gem). However we label it, editing out what no longer serves us is one of the most cathartic and healing efforts we can initiate, and that applies to our relationships as well. (Just a little personal coaching thrown in with your decorating tip.)

Make The Most Out Of Your Doors And Moldings

This question always comes up with my telephone Design Mentor clients: "Once I've decided to paint my walls, what color should I paint the woodwork?" Before I answer, I usually ask a few more questions, for example, are the moldings and doors currently painted or stained a natural wood stain? Is the style you're after traditional or contemporary? What's the condition of the current moldings and doors? If you opt to paint the woodwork in one room, will you feel you have to carry through and paint the woodwork throughout all of the rooms in your entire house? Usually, the answers to these questions point in one direction or another.

Painting your moldings

In general, traditional décor lends itself to white or creamy off-white woodwork and moldings. If your house has particularly beautiful moldings, such as elaborate fluted crown-moldings, wainscoting, and chair rails, of course you should highlight this woodwork with a color that contrasts with your walls. And if you have colorful walls (by now I've convinced you that this is a good idea, right?), the best way to contrast would be with white or ivory, depending on the tone of your wall color (see page 23, Warm and Cool Palettes).

If the woodwork, on the other hand, is pretty plain and otherwise unattractive, the best way to *not* call attention to it is to paint it the same color as the walls. If your taste tends toward the contemporary, again blending the woodwork with the color on the walls is more typical.

For a whimsical, artsy, or unusual treatment, boldly painted walls look fun and funky with a different bold color on the trim (see photo).

And remember, while you may choose to paint your walls a satin or eggshell finish, it's generally recommended that you paint your doors and moldings in a gloss or semi-gloss finish. Both semi-gloss and gloss paints adhere particularly well to wood, are easy to clean, and will help protect the wood from the invariable scratches and nicks moldings tend to receive from furniture (and humans!).

Staining your wood moldings

Stained wood moldings (versus painted moldings) is a particular look. Many homes built in the seventies are filled with stained dark woodwork. Conversely, many homes built in the early twentieth century are filled with beautiful gleaming woodwork, also stained in dark tones. This is a personal choice as to whether you like this look, or find it too dated or heavy. While many of my colleagues may disagree, I see nothing intrinsically wrong with painting the moldings and woodwork in some rooms, while leaving other rooms stained and natural. The most important thing is to have the woodwork contribute to the overall theme you're trying express in each room.

Adding moldings

If you're in a home that doesn't have moldings, installing them will add character and definition to an otherwise plain room. You should, however, fully consider if you're willing to add molding throughout the entire house, or just in the most public rooms, i.e., rooms used for entertaining. Ideally, if you're going to add moldings, you should commit to adding them throughout the house, so they look original to the house, and don't appear to be an afterthought. Remember, if

In this, my vibrant and stimulating home office, we opted to paint the moldings a shade of orange sherbet, which nicely complimented the pinky coral walls. Everything about this space is lively and whimsical, so the colors fit right in.

you tend to like a contemporary, more streamlined look in your home, molding isn't really consistent with this look, so save your money and skip the molding. Consider another dramatic way to infuse character in the public rooms, such as adding a striking cable or track light.

A final consideration about molding involves ceiling height. If you opt to add molding in your home and like the traditional look of painting it off-white or white, in contrast to your wall colors, be aware that molding visually brings your eyes down. If you have high ceilings, this is the effect you want; it will add a cozy, less cavernous feel to the room. However, if your ceilings are low to begin with (seven feet, for example), painted molding will just add to the existing crowded feeling low ceilings bring to a room.

Window trim, chair rails, crown molding – all can be wonderful architectural elements in your home. Just fully consider how you want to dress them if you have them in your home, and if you don't, ask yourself if adding them is worth the expense and the design statement you'll be making.

In this stately 1800s Mansard Colonial home, the moldings are among the most beautiful details. We purposely kept the window treatments to a minimum so as not to hide the fluted moldings; we then highlighted them by painting them out in creamy linen white. The contrast to the brick red wallpaper is striking and dramatic.

Part III:
Special Situations

Here you'll find "special wisdom," otherwise known as answers to unrelated but nonetheless important questions. These topics could easily occupy the better part of an entire book, and maybe that will be my sequel someday! But for now, I wanted to give you some assistance if you're daunted by issues such as living in a condo, or decorating beautifully in a small space. Again, these topics come up frequently in my work and are worth addressing.

Another topic that's particularly popular these days is the importance of readying your home for sale. On the West Coast, *staging*, as it's called, is an art form practiced by many specially-trained professionals. Staging involves any and all efforts undertaken to improve and declutter the overall appearance of one's home, thereby increasing the probability that it sells quickly and garners a high asking price. In my conservative New England region, the profession hasn't blossomed yet. But I'm happy to see that homeowners have finally caught on to the fact that, with effort and guidance, they can take on this project themselves. I've written extensively on this topic, so if you're getting ready to move, read on! Even if you're not contemplating a move, you may find this section illuminating. The benefits always far outweigh the effort; I even knew a woman who changed her mind about moving after we put her home in selling condition!

Finally, I've given suggestions for changing your interiors with the changing seasons, while encouraging you to get outside and enjoy what Mother Nature has to offer.

Hopefully these tips will help you address your special spaces, both indoors and out, and make your home and garden places you'll hate to leave.

Give Small Spaces A Bigger Feel

Small spaces are a particularly hard challenge for many of us, because we all have so much stuff! But I can assure you they have the potential to look as great as any larger space if you keep some key considerations in mind:

• *Do not* feel like you have to paint all of your walls white. Paint colors from the mid-range of most color fans look stunning and dramatic in small spaces, as long as you make other space-saving efforts.

• Don't mix various shades of wood. While most large rooms can handle this eclecticism, in a small space, it looks too busy. Stick to one tone of wood for all pieces. This ideally includes the wood frames on your artwork as well.

• Consider painting unattractive bookshelves the same color as the walls. The effect will look like custom built-ins, instead of mismatched furniture.

• Very important: Purchase pieces that serve dual functions, such as a blanket chest that does double duty as a coffee table or a breakfast bar in the kitchen that can be used as a cooking prep space.

• Try to purchase pieces that are rollable, stackable, or nestable for optimal flexibility and optimized storage usage.

In this diminutive 250-square-foot beach cottage, most pieces served dual function: the breakfast bar doubled as a cooking prep space, the coffee table doubled as a blanket chest, and of course, the sofa opened up to become a sleeper. A rosy white paint was the perfect backdrop for the inspired hues of blue, coral pink, and tan.

• When it comes to accessories, think quality, not quantity. Choose your accessories judiciously, because small spaces require only a few accessories that carry a big punch. Your personality needs to be expressed with less in a small space. This includes window treatments. Small spaces aren't the place to hang yards and yards of heavy fabrics, or dark-stained wood blinds for that matter.

• Watch how many patterns and prints you bring into your small space. Keep your largest furnishings solid and save the patterns and prints for artwork and accessories such as pillows and vases.

• While we're on the subject of "small," group small objects together. Small items such as vases, miniature figurines, etc. will have far greater impact

grouped together rather than scattered all over the house. Additionally, place these small collections on a small-scale surface, such as a small table or wall étagère. Small treasures are easily overshadowed by larger items if they share the same space.

• If you just can't part with the items that don't fit in your current space, consider renting a storage garage nearby. The nominal monthly fee is worth the feeling of comfort you'll feel daily in your uncluttered small digs.

And perhaps, first and foremost, *plan* and think about how you'll really live in this small space. For example, don't be seduced into buying a massive sub-zero refrigerator just because it's in vogue if you rarely cook and always order take-out. Small spaces tolerate less purchasing mishaps than do large rooms, so think well before you buy. A little forethought will go a long way. Living with just what you need and not a lot of extra clutter may make you feel a little like Henry David Thoreau. But you just might discover what he and many small space-dwellers already know: We all can easily get by with less.

This space was originally designed to be the eat–in kitchen area of this house, yet even a small table and four chairs were awkward, blocking traffic flow to the bathroom (door shown). Solution: extending the peninsula from the kitchen and adding three bar stools for casual eating instead of the table. A roll-top desk for managing household finances was added, along with a sweet window seat, which provided extra storage underneath, and custom seat cushion and matching window valance. Don't feel limited by your small spaces – get creative!

Fresh bath towels that have never been used go a long way to create the neat and tidy look you want in your bath when company drops in. Keep them in a special place that's easily accessible.

Low-stress Entertaining With A "Company's Coming" Kit

So now my secret's out. We love to entertain, be it an intimate dinner party with four couples, or a casual and festive holiday potluck with our twenty best friends, affectionately known as "The Core." When an event is planned in advance, of course, we schedule adequate time to do a thorough cleaning to vacuum up feline hairballs and the stray pepper seeds leftover from last night's supper. But what about when company is coming on short notice? Like when a client decides to swing by and pick up those fabric samples that just arrived, and of course, I'll ask her to stay for coffee. Or when my designer colleagues (a.k.a. the Decorating Divas) with whom I meet monthly decide to meet at my house this month? I really don't want to launch a full-scale cleaning effort, but I do want the house to look more presentable. My answer: I pull out my emergency "Company's Coming" satchel. In it, you'll find a variety of "fixes" such as:

1. *A full roll of toilet paper.* I remove the typically almost-empty roll and replace it with the new roll.

2. *Two freshly folded bath towels*. These are large towels I never use for any other purpose so they never stain or wear out. Isn't it nicer for a guest to brush up against a dry towel rather than one that's wet and hanging on the family towel bar from the morning showers? Hang the wet ones in the basement.

3. *Two delicate and unstained finger towels.* The big bath towels above are really more for draping over the towel racks. The finger towels are what the guests actually use to dry their hands.

4. *A can of elegant potpourri spray.* This means I hide the 99-cent can of air freshener and put out the good stuff! Oh yea, I spray the good stuff throughout the house before I place it on the bathroom counter. (Um, side note: never, repeat *never*, leave matches for scenting the bathroom. Who decided that the smell of burning sulfur was preferable to you-know-what?) Oh, and I make sure to empty the bathroom waste basket.

5. *A fake fur throw:* I confess, I casually drape this on my side of the bed to hide the pulls on the duvet caused by my kitties' claws.

Finally, I remove all of the throws on my living room chairs that we use daily to protect the chairs from kitty hair. I could never live without my (husband and) cats, but many of my guests are very sensitive to their fur. So it's far easier to simply remove the furry throws than to rigorously vacuum the chairs.

You get the idea, right? Nobody lives with their homes in a "perpetually company-ready" state, so don't fight it. But make it easy on yourself by having an emergency kit nearby, so you'll be ready and unstressed when they do drop by on short notice.

Stylin' Furnishings For Our Furry Friends

This crisp slipcover will catch spills and tolerate kitty hair while still looking presentable. When company's coming, simply whip it off and drop it in the wash. Your furnishings underneath will remain clean and hairless as you get ready to greet your guests!

In case I haven't mentioned it yet, I'm a huge animal lover, most specifically ones with fur (which includes my husband). While a sweet tenant of mine named Louise was the consummate Dr. Dolittle with five pets, including her eighteen-inch-long pet iguana, I happen to be partial to mammals. And luckily for all animal lovers, it just so happens that pet furniture and accessories have been elevated to a new fashion high in recent years.

While I must confess I don't own any high-tech or high-style pet furnishings, I feel obligated to mention some of the items that are now available for our furry best friends.

You can find a myriad of options of stylish pet beds on a variety of websites dedicated to pampering our pets. Believe it or not, your pet can snooze in his or her very own futon, or better yet, canopy bed made with an antique finish wrought iron frame. You can order the cushions in shaggy chenille, fake fur, or my favorite, a wild leopard print. If minimalism is more your design aesthetic, you'll be happy to know that websites also exist that specialize in both furniture and accessories that reflect the clean lines and subdued colors of both modern and post-modern styles. With all the wonderful websites out there that carry items for pets, you'll have no trouble finding accessories that not only function well for your pet, but that fit in with your décor.

Our kitties have simple tastes; a soft and cushy cat bed is more than adequate for Lilly and Henley, taken in a rare moment when they aren't rumbling and are actually sharing the bed.

If high style pet furnishings are too over the top for you, *and* your pet prefers to sleep on your sofa anyway, you can go the simple route of purchasing slipcovers for your furnishings. Again, a simple browse around the Internet will turn up a great selection of well-priced styles of slipcovers for any décor. If you're really a no-nonsense type of decorator, visit your local home fashions department store and purchase inexpensive fleece throws for covering your sofa and chairs. They are easy to launder and can quickly be removed when guests arrive unexpectedly. With not a pet hair to be found, your guests will walk in and say, "Wow, I thought you said you had pets?" You can often find fleece throws that match the color of your furnishings so they will blend more with the décor of the room. These are always better than covering your furnishings with sheets, which makes your house look like no one has lived there for thirty years.

Aside from purchasing furniture designed for pets, there are a few other things you can do to maintain the beauty of your home and minimize the abuse to your possessions that inevitably occurs with these treasured creatures. For starters, if you own cats, include a scratching post or two in your home. Even kitties who have been declawed will intuitively continue this behavior and you'd probably prefer their little litterbox-digging foot pads to be rubbing the scratch pad and not your white silk settee. And

I have found that providing your kitties with yummy cat grass is a great way to keep them from chewing on your houseplants. Henley is about to dig in to his Christmas present.

dog owners: You already know that a house devoid of chew toys is a house replete with chew marks, specifically on all of the wood legs of your tables and chairs, not to mention your base cove moldings and your favorite black stilettos.

When purchasing furniture for the house, try to avoid loose weave fabrics such as buckram, chenille, houndstooth, and tapestries, to name a few. They are most likely to get snagged by your animal's claws. On the other hand, polished cottons, chintz, denim, and fabrics with at least twenty-five percent polyester will resist such pulls. Wicker furniture will also tend to attract felines who feel the urge to sharpen their claws or canines that need a good chew.

Finally, when pets miss their target or just can't wait 'til Mummy or Daddy arrive home from work, nothing works like chlorine bleach on your *hard* surfaces *only* to remove stubborn pet odors. When it comes to soiled

This homeowner was fortunate enough to find throws that perfectly matched her chaise lounge, since no soft surface is off-limits to Daisy.

fabrics, there are many products now available that are specifically designed to remove pet odors and stains from carpet and fabric. Some even offer the added benefit of helping to remove pet hair imbedded in fabric. You can liberally sprinkle products onto the carpet before you vacuum your pet's favorite nap spot; they really lift the hair and smell wonderful and fresh – wow, what a concept!

If you feel the way I do, which is to say you cannot imagine life without your pets, you'll want to take a few steps to make your home as pet-friendly as possible. And now it's possible to include them in the overall design scheme as well.

In this condo kitchen, my client invested in recessed lights. Between the recessed lights on a dimmer and the fan light, she has an adequate supply of both task and ambient lighting.

Yes, You Can Have A Stunningly Stylish Condo

I frequently receive requests on my website to speak on the "How-To's" of condo decorating. Often clients feel they won't be living in their condos for very long, and thus want suggestions that are purely decorative (i.e., portable) and not structural. Others find the open floor plan of many new condos a challenge, wondering where to end one paint color and begin another! So I thought I'd share some decorating wisdom that will help make your condo a warm and inviting nest for as little or as long as you choose to roost!

• *Bring in color.* So many newer condos are bathed in beige, from the countertops to the floor tiles. This is usually done for easy resale but can be pretty bland for living. Think about your favorite two or three colors and work them into each room. A very popular color trio is butternut yellow, burgundy, and celadon green. If you prefer earthier tones, try cappuccino tan, celadon green, and deep mocha. Go to town with colored linens, accessories, and of course paint.

• *Speaking of paint...* As I stated on page 110, nothing transforms the look and feel of a space for less time, energy, and cash than painting the walls. Feel free to paint two or three colors in the living space of those condos that have open floor plans. This is *very* in style. Just ensure two things: (1) That the colors you choose are of the same intensity, i.e., that they are roughly on the same step on the color fan, and (2) that you make sure you have a definite stopping point, such as the end of a wall, before you change paint color. You can paint butternut yellow on two walls in your dining room, and mocha on the adjacent wall that wraps around to the hallway. Just don't change colors in the middle of an archway (yes, I have seen this...).

• *Use area rugs to hide sins.* If your condo is plagued with (beige!) wall-to-wall carpet that's tired, old, or otherwise stained, consider adding area rugs. You can add a 6x9-foot or 8x10-foot area rug under your dining room set, a 5x7-foot in front of the couch, and several runners in the hallways and around the beds. Area rugs are available in all price points these days (see page 60 for more on area rugs), so you should be able to find something that fits your needs exactly. Before you make a large investment in a new area

rug, however, decide if you love your current furnishings. If you think you'll keep your basic couch and chairs, dining room set, and existing bed linens if you move, then you may want to purchase a better-than-average area rug that will last. However, if you're in a transitional phase of your life, save your pennies and consider buying bargain area rugs now, as you may find your style and preferences have changed considerably by the time you move again. When you're in a more permanent home you can invest in all new furnishings and rugs.

This same client, determined to stay a long while in this condo, made it her own by adding bright and fanciful wallpaper in a French Provincial style. Notice the addition of the portable maple island that offers much-needed, and attractive, storage.

• *Purchase a kitchen island.* Many condos have limited counter space, but older buildings that have been converted to condos often have enormous floor space! Since you'd probably rather cook than dance in this kitchen, consider a stand-alone island. A far cry from the butcher-block islands of the seventies, today's islands often resemble stunning pieces of furniture, with carved legs, built-in wine racks, and shelves equipped with wicker cubbies. A four- or five-foot long island will store a large assortment of bowls, utensils, and groceries (ideally stored in a wicker hamper and covered with a kitchen towel) *and* will give you another expanse of prep area.

• *Let there be light.* If your condo isn't equipped with overhead lighting, let me say two things. (1) While all of the afore-mentioned tips are designed to be portable fixes, it's actually a very good investment to consider adding recessed lights. They will only enhance the look and value of your unit when you choose to sell. (2) However, if you're dead-set against making any permanent changes, then you must add light through lamps (pole and table) and with the use of mirrors. Have at least three sources of light in every room, and try to avoid placing a torchiere-type light (one that shoots light upwards) on a wall that's dinged or otherwise has imperfections, as it will highlight all of the flaws on the surface on which it shines. If you have great window space, place a mirror opposite the windows; it will bounce the natural light around your condo, really brightening it up!

• *Choose the correct furnishings.* Often newer condos have large living rooms, which are an open invitation to purchase sectionals. Sectionals are plush and comfy and usually enormous. If you sell your condo and gleefully purchase a bungalow or Colonial single family home, you may have to leave your sectional on the curb. Consider purchasing couches, loveseats, and club chairs to fill a room, rather than a sectional, as these pieces are all much more versatile in the long-term. If you're blessed with a very large living room, try angling the furniture. Angling is very hip and stylish and, as I mentioned earlier in the book, is actually not the best utilization of space. This is what you want in an oversized room, rather than having to purchase more furnishings to fill the space.

So whether your condo is designed to house you temporarily, or in fact, you love its maintenance-free lifestyle and plan to stay for the long haul, beautiful and functional design décor can indeed be yours!

These folks put out hanging decorations for a party and decided to leave them up for their open house. The effect is neat, tidy, and festive.

Perk Up Your House For A Quick Sale!

So much attention has been given to this popular topic. Without a doubt, the better you can present your home, the more likely a potential buyer will recognize its benefits. I've broken down my suggestions into three categories: simple cosmetic changes, more in-depth changes for the interior, and changes to the exterior of your house.

Interior uplift

These are changes you can do for little or no money; they may just take a little of your time. But think of this as time you would have spent packing for your move anyway – you're just getting an extra benefit for all your hard work!

• *Drastically reduce clutter.* Recycle old newspapers, file away bill receipts (pay those bills that are due!), and dispose of old magazines or gather them in wicker baskets and place beside a reading chair. Put away all piles of clothing, or better yet, if you haven't worn an item for at least two years, donate it to your favorite charity. If you still have too many objects for the space, consider renting a local storage garage. It will be well worth the money.

• *Replace linens.* In your kitchen, replace worn, ripped, or stained dishtowels and pot holders with fresh and colorful linens purchased at a discount store. If your tablecloths are in rough shape, consider replacing them. Fruit patterns are very popular and lush for the kitchen; lace or solid moirés are elegant in the dining room. Update your dining room by bringing in an exotic Far Eastern element with the addition of a sheer embroidered tablecloth with or without sequins and small beads.

Notice how clean and empty her countertops are? Rule No. 1 in staging: declutter!

• *Examine your counters.* Put dirty, greasy, or old-looking spice jars and bottles of oil in the cupboard. Display only clean decorative jars and bottles. Beautiful decanters of pickled fruits and vegetables, as well as vinegars and oils, can be purchased almost anywhere. Boxes of cereal, cookies, breads, and jars of peanut butter and commonly used condiments should all go back in the cupboard.

• *Create a lovely display.* Fresh fruit in a pottery or ceramic pasta bowl makes a lovely still life on your kitchen table or countertop. Just make sure your over-ripened fruit is put in the refrigerator or tossed.

• *Follow your nose!* Whenever possible, during a showing or an open house have potpourri burners going (ask your realtor to tend to this detail). Or better yet, use a variety of home fragrance products such as "plug-in" oil and gel packs that don't require any tending. Vanilla and cinnamon apple are great in the kitchen; light florals are great in other rooms. And change these scents with the season. Also, never underestimate the power of beautiful and fragrant potted plants or bouquets of cut flowers for open houses. Flowers are like chocolate; who doesn't immediately feel happy in their presence?

• *Jazz up your bathroom.* Try to display only "guest towels" at all times. Take the wet, just-used bath towels and drape them in the basement. Don't display toothpaste, dental floss, prescriptions, or other personal toiletries. Remove all cleaning supplies from view. Do display attractively wrapped soaps in small baskets and decorative decanters. If your bathroom is light enough, consider adding a small green plant on the tank of the toilet; this is also good Feng Shui.

• *Corral the toys.* If you have children, collect all the scattered toys from throughout the house and place them in baskets or colored storage bins. Consider purchasing a "hanging net" that suspends between two adjacent walls to hold small and lightweight stuffed animals.

Bigger changes for a bigger payoff
Beyond simple cosmetic changes, it may be very worthwhile to do the following in your home:

• *Perk up your floors.* Stained wall-to-wall carpet is a big turnoff. Replacing the carpet with fresh neutral beige is always a good idea. If there's hardwood underneath, even better. You can't lose by exposing hardwood floors, and if necessary, spending the money to re-sand and -finish them. If there are no deep gouges or scrapes, you might be able to get by with "screening" the floors, which is a much lighter sanding and therefore a less-expensive version of refinishing.

• *Add neutral colors.* While I'm a big fan of bold color on the walls, it's often too personal a statement for a buyer to digest. Consider painting over your colorful walls, again in a soft beige or cream color. Examine the trim on your windows and baseboard. If it's chipped and nicked, it's worth sanding and repainting in a gloss finish. This makes a big difference in the overall quality of a room.

• *Light things up.* What kind of lighting does the home have? Many homes from the seventies are filled with track lighting with heads the size of footballs. Consider replacing track lighting with lovely and discrete recessed lights. Also, dated ceiling-mounted light fixtures can really detract from the house. Consider replacing these with affordable and stylish new ones, which are readily available at any of the national home supply chain stores.

• *Rooms with plumbing merit extra attention.* Kitchens and baths are really important areas to examine; these are often the deal-makers or -breakers in a sale, so every penny you put into fixing up these rooms will come back to you. Try one or more of these improvements:

  • Flooring: Old, dirty, and scratched linoleum absolutely should be replaced. If you can afford it, consider replacing unappealing floors with neutral ceramic tile. If your budget is tighter, linoleum peel-and-stick tiles will work wonders. If by some awful chance you have carpet in your kitchen or bath, absolutely replace this.

If you saw this attractive display on a porch, wouldn't you be invited to walk in and see the rest of the house? I can't say enough about the importance of curb appeal.

  • Countertops: If they are tile and the grout is stained, you should scrub it with bleach. If the old grout is permanently stained, it's worth the elbow grease to scrape up most of the old grout and re-grout with new product. If your laminate countertops are cracked, nicked, or scratched, consider replacing these with a fresh and stylish laminate,

All these years I thought this smiling chap was Buddha; he is actually known as the Jolly Hotei, the Japanese God of Happiness. What better place to put him than at your front entrance to greet your guests?

also in a neutral color that goes with the décor. Laminates are now designed to look very much like authentic marble and granite.

• Cabinets: If they're worn, scratched, cracked, or have broken hinges, this will really turn off a buyer. If they are light-colored wood, perhaps you'll only have to sand and re-stain them. If they are very dark and heavy-looking (circa 1970), it's worth sanding, priming, and painting them in a fresh white or cream color. Add new hardware from this millennium and your kitchen will be reborn.

• Faucets: This is an inexpensive but powerful fix. Replacing pieces that are tarnished, pitted, or oxidized with bright new faucets will make your entire kitchen or bathroom look cleaner and brighter. Make sure you buy faucets that match the spread of the existing ones (four- or eight-inch).

Exterior changes – wow 'em as they walk in

Making sure your exterior is beautiful and tidy is just as important as your interior for buyers. You want to make sure your curb appeal really draws the potential buyers in! Here are some ideas for changes you can implement, in order of difficulty/expense:

• Unclutter your yard by removing scattered toys, garden supplies and empty pots, runaway garden hoses, etc. Pack them neatly in bins and store out of sight, in a basement, shed, or garage.

• Space permitting, add a pretty garden statue to welcome guests, such as a *Jolly Hotei*!

• If you already have a thousand tchochkies in your yard and on your porch – get rid of all of it, except those items mentioned in this list!

• Replace a rusted or damaged mailbox.

• Replace any dirty or torn welcome mats and worn or broken porch or yard furniture. Make sure you substitute these items *only* with attractive pieces.

• Remove *all* dead plants and bushes and add plantings that bring in texture and color. Remove overgrown weeds from all gardens and from in between cement walkways.

• Climate permitting, hang or display interesting and attractive plants in pretty containers on decks or porches.

• Replace tarnished or dated exterior light fixtures in the yard and on your house.

• Re-seed or re-sod an unattractive lawn or patches of dried grass and keep the lawn mowed and tidy.

• Power wash your house, *unless* you feel the paint is in too shaky a condition and will peel.

• Fix cracks on plaster/stucco exteriors and paint.

Whether you decide to do a little or a lot, any changes you do will pay off in dividends. Some is better than nothing, and in this case, more is best. Are you unsure if your home is really that bad and needs any of these improvements? I mean, how bad could it be, right? It's virtually impossible to step outside of ourselves and see our homes objectively. You may want to ask a dear friend whose constructive criticism you can tolerate (and with whom you share a strong enough friendship) to come in and talk candidly about the condition of your home prior to your listing it. Go through this list with him or her and be prepared to hear tough love. When your house sells for the price you're asking, or even greater, you'll instantly be reminded of the wonderful value of true friends. Hop to it – there's money to be made!

Bring furnishings closer together, turn on some soft lighting, and light a roaring fire: let it snow, let it snow, let it snow.

Change Your Home With The Seasons: Hunkering Down For The Winter…

I'm a lifelong New Englander who, for better or worse, has always known the glory of the four seasons. I have very sweet childhood memories of watching both my mother and grandmother change the living and dining room draperies to welcome in the new season every spring and fall. It was a tradition practiced by generations gone by that has all but fallen by the wayside.

Despite the changing of homemakers' rituals and the variety of regional climates, I regularly get emails from people asking for ways to help make their homes feel cozier in the winter. While you begin your autumn and winter holiday decorating, why not consider adding additional warmth and coziness to your interiors that will comfort you even after the holidays are over? Here are a few easy ways:

• **Dress up your windows.** Hang sumptuous velvet or brocade panels to your windows by adding a second curtain rod, or by flanking them alongside your airy sheers. Or if you prefer the look of casually draped yards of fabrics, replace your filmy linen and sheer fabric window scarves with yards of burnt velvet or soft chenille. Letting the scarves puddle to the floor adds extra drama and richness.

• *Bring out the heavy wool area rugs.* Many of my clients like the cool and smooth feel of bare hardwood floors under their feet in the warmer weather. Now is definitely the time to add insulation and texture by bringing back the richness of wool area rugs. If you currently have wall-to-wall broadloom, an area rug will add color and new style placed right over it, either in front of the coffee table or along the sides and at the end of your bed. Very plush, very cozy!

In this eclectic parlor, we added voluminous drapes and cozy throws for the cooler months. They not only physically provide insulation against the cold but visually provide a warmer, more cozy sensibility.

• *Pull your furnishings closer together.* We now want to focus more on hunkering down and nesting. Especially if you have a fireplace, there's nothing that says winter more than friends gathering around a crackling fire sipping brandy (herbal tea?), sitting close to each other. If you don't already own some, invest in a few soft chenille throws.

• *Change the scent of your home.* Home-scenting has never been more popular than it is today. In October and November, I break out all of my cool-weather scents such as cinnamon, spiced pumpkin, and gingerbread. The day after Thanksgiving, without fail, I put out the holly berry, sugar cookie, and balsam scents. And these days, you can find scents in a plethora of forms, including candles, sprays, potpourri, and "plug in" oils and gel packs.

• *"Winterize" your accessories.* Many interiors lend themselves to both a "light and bright" as well as "deep and rich" interpretation of their color scheme. Look at your silk centerpieces, interior wreathes, candles, pillows, tablecloths, and throws. If they are expressing "summer" more than "winter," it's time to change. For example, consider replacing your soft sage, lemon yellow, and mauve floral arrangement with one that is olive, butternut, and claret. I would bet the deeper arrangement will look just as lovely, and more seasonally appropriate.

So whether you live in a region that lives with six months of snow, or your idea of winter is when the thermometer registers forty-degrees, whenever the chill begins to fill the air, we intuitively want to hunker down, cuddle up, and metaphorically start hibernating. This coming autumn, don't fight your instincts; honor them and give yourself what you crave: a warm and cozy sanctuary to keep you sheltered until after the storm. (Or, as in the case of New England, until after the last of *many* storms!)

During the cooler months, this den is filled with bean bag chairs and heavy wool area rugs for the kids. Come springtime, it becomes Mom's sunny retreat with crisp white wicker and floral window treatments. Sorry kids, go play outside.

Change Your Home With The Seasons: Warm Weather Is Coming...

In New England, it isn't always easy to tell when spring has arrived. I mean, I do see the crocuses popping through patches of snow and eventually the daffodils make an appearance, but snowstorms followed by really raw and cold rain often characterizes our spring until June. Nonetheless, I'm not daunted; as soon as Mother Nature allows, I start my rituals. Here are a few things you can do change your home for the coming of warmer weather, and fellow New Englanders: Fear not, it always comes.

• *Lighten up your windows.* Replace heavy window treatments with lighter versions. If the view is pleasant, leave the windows bare or dressed only in privacy shades/blinds. If you like more textiles, consider dressing the windows in light and filmy panels or sheers voluminously draped over a rod. Place a bird's nest and artificial bird in one of the drapes of the filmy fabric for a whimsical touch!

• *Remove those heavy wool area rugs.* Consider replacing these with either lighter cotton throw rugs, or keep the heft of wool, but choose rugs that are lighter in hue and theme. Botanicals and playful geometric prints are a nice warm weather alternative to the serious heaviness of winter's oriental rugs. Alternately, you can leave your floors bare; especially if you have hardwood floors, the bare wood can feel nice and cool on your feet in the summer.

• *Invest in a nice set of slipcovers.* There are now catalogs and websites devoted entirely to nothing but slipcovers! Having slipcovers in lighter shades for warm weather and darker shades for cool weather guarantees two things: (1) Your rooms will instantly take on the look of the new season and (2) your furniture will last twice as long. *And* most are washable!

This client says this is the closest thing to bathing outside. In the warm weather, we remove the heavy drapery panels and fuzzy area rugs and let the sunshine pour in.

• *Create space between your furnishings.* We want to focus less on hunkering down and nesting, and more on expanding and breathing the fresh new air of the season. More space between furnishings is visually uplifting, and it physically frees up energy and allows it to circulate. When temperatures allow, throw open the windows and cleanse away the stale winter air.

• *Bring some real flowers indoors.* There's nothing like the smell of forced narcissus bulbs to foreshadow spring. And if they are a bit too heady for you, stop in at the supermarket and bring home inexpensive bouquets of daffodils, hyacinths, or tulips. Your mood will begin to improve, I promise you.

• *Change the scent of your home.* As I discussed earlier, scent is a powerful way to define your home's personality. As the weather warms up, we intuitively want to start smelling light floral scents like lilac and daylily, or wonderful fruity aromas like pear and tangerine. These scents are just strong enough to freshen up your house's atmosphere, while not being too heavy for the warm weather.

Finally, now that the sun starts to grace the morning sky at increasingly early hours, view it as a gift that you don't want to miss. Rise earlier and tackle the things you never seem to get to once the family rises. *Or* simply spend this hour alone with your mug of coffee quietly and excitedly contemplating your next bold move.

Every spring I am absolutely tickled to see bird couples flying in and out of the birdhouses we put out for them. I think of them as our extended family (yes, I have been called odd at times).

Make Your Yard An Extension Of Your Home

Walking around in my backyard this past weekend really inspired me to think about the not-to-be-underestimated value of communing with nature. I could never be characterized as the outdoorsy type; in fact my official winter sport is mall-trolling. However, over the years, I've come to realize that meditation for me (if not shopping) is truly spending time sitting quietly outside, watching and listening to nature at work. So whether you're lucky enough to enjoy tepid temperatures year round, or like me, have to make hay while the sun shines in late spring, summer, and early fall, consider bringing the gentility and comfort of the great indoors outside to your yard.

Many of you who live in a hot climate year-round are fully versed on the fabulous concept of outdoor living, with open-air kitchens and lanais (a.k.a. porches or verandas). For the rest of you, here are a few simple things you can do to your yard that will increase your pleasure for those precious months when you're able to enjoy it.

• *Paint your lawn furniture bright colors.* Whether you like the dazzle of red, blue, and yellow primary hues or the luscious brights of periwinkle, raspberry, and kiwi green, paint your wood Adirondack chairs and benches in bright tones. They will fill your garden with color, especially if your flower gardens are being installed over time, are immature, and don't provide a lot of color on their own. And with new high-tech spray paints, you can even paint your plastic lawn furniture any color you want, which will really allow you to customize the colors in your backyard, much like you would in your interior space.

Before I made all my cats indoors-only, Zachary could be regularly found nestled in the tulip garden also communing with Mother Nature.

• *Make yourself an elegant dining spot.* Find an area in your yard that is naturally canopied by trees, and set up an informal table and some chairs. An inexpensive ice cream parlor set will work just fine. Hang a wrought iron chandelier overhead from a sturdy branch and light with candles (make sure they are far away from foliage with the open flame!). Add a casual tablecloth and a handful of candle cups and you're ready to dine alfresco.

• *Bring words of wisdom to your garden.* Consider adding decorative tile pavers throughout the walkways and destinations of your yard. You can find them with lovely sayings and affirmations carved into them such as "Grow old with me, the best is yet to be." For a jolt of color, they are also available with ceramic tiles and stained glass laid across the top.

• *Add a birdbath.* My mood has been known to shift from grumpy to happy in an instant if I catch a glimpse of birds flapping around in the birdbath in my backyard. Keep it clean and full of fresh water. You'll be doing Mother Nature a favor by caring for her small creatures and you just might find your mood start to improve.

• *Add comfy furniture.* If you're lucky enough to have a screened-in porch, consider wicker. Wicker is the classic warm weather furniture that immediately conjures up images of lounging in Baton Rouge while sipping lemonade (or a mint julep!). Wicker will add instant character, but, if placed outside, will eventually show its wear from the elements. If you really want your furniture to last, consider purchasing the widely-available "wicker resin" pieces. This is a glamorous term for plastic, but it looks and feels like the real thing, and will last much longer in the elements than natural wicker. For those of you who will be adding porch furniture to your deck, consider investing in a deck storage chest. You can purchase these at any home-improvement store for under $100. They will hold your seat cushions and outdoor pillows and protect them from both the blistering sun and pelting rain. Won't it be nice to dine alfresco and not have to sit on a squishy wet seat cushion? You may also want to consider inexpensive furniture covers for your larger pieces, which come in many shapes and sizes. These are usually easy to slip on and off of your tables and chairs and will increase the longevity of your outdoor furniture.

Finally, if at all possible, find two sturdy trees that are about fifteen feet apart and hang a hammock. I bought one for my husband for his birthday last year and he adores it. I've fallen asleep on it more times than I can count. From this lazy vantage point, you can gaze at your growing flower gardens, watch the birds frolic in their bath, and despite what you wish you had more of, practice being thankful for all of the abundance and beauty in your life.

Because I'm Italian, I can get away with calling this a "Guido Ball," technically called a Gazing Ball. My husband protested when I wanted to buy this several years ago but immediately loved it when it reached our garden. Where I grew up, every self-respecting Italian family had one – c'mon join the club; share the love.

I couldn't resist sharing with you my view from the hammock. It's positively serene.

Parting Wisdom

You know, I think it was Confucius who said that if you do what you love, you'll never work another day in your life. A truer statement has never been spoken. I feel blessed every day to be able to do what I love; the fact that I also get paid to do it is just icing on the cake. I hope you found this book helpful – maybe even inspiring – and will take the next step: action! Whether you're trying to learn piano, master a tricky dance step, or work up the nerve to paint your bedroom, few things are as exhilarating as taking a chance and changing yourself in some measurable way. In this case, the results are more wide-reaching than simply having painted walls; there's no doubt in my mind that taking small steps and doing something different (or out of character) is highly empowering.

My goal in writing this book was to offer you simple – and sometimes stunning – ways to make changes; to introduce new ways for you to surround yourself with beauty and richness that truly honors your spirit and feeds your soul. And if your spirit calls for bold colors and lively patterns, fabulous. Or maybe your spirit is contemplative and cerebral, and craves the peace and calm of a neutral interior with minimal accessories – that's lovely too. So whatever you want your home to express, now is the time to go and honor this. Your interiors should reflect your authentic self and that, my friends, is what spiritual decorating is all about. It actually isn't about hanging yin/yang symbols everywhere or bringing statues of Buddha into your space. It is about surrounding yourself with objects that make your heart sing. If you live in someone else's idea of a beautiful interior, or worse, an interior filled with memories of a difficult past, it's time to change. If I may paraphrase Heracles: It is in change that we find purpose.

Like any good mentor, I hope I've been successful in encouraging both action and change. And if in the event my book has whet your appetite and you would like one-on-one structured direction from a design therapist, remember, there's always Design Mentor. I've worked with people from as far away as Australia and Romania. I would love to meet you!

If just keeping in touch sounds good, I invite you to sign up for my decorating Tip of the Month, through my website, RenaissanceInteriorDesign.com. I value your feedback, so please feel free to drop me a line.

Until we meet again, I wish you love and light,

Jayne Pelosi

Acknowledgements

This is the part of the book where a novice author such as myself has to resist the temptation to thank everyone I ever met and was ever nice to me. What if I never write another book (although Paige, my publicist and Public Relations Guru will never allow that to happen)… What if this is my one and only chance of acknowledging the hundreds, maybe thousands, of special people who contributed to the person I am today?

Relax. I'll try to keep the list bearable. In a moment, I'll mention the team of brilliant souls who made the creation of this book a reality. Right now, however, I can't help but think of a few faces from a very long time ago who left an imprint on my life.

I thank Mr. Robert Cleasby, my tenth grade choral director, who encouraged me to sing and brought music to a newer, more personal level in my life, which was quite a feat considering I grew up with a tenor sax player for a father. While it's probable that I'll never sing professionally, participating in music and music theatre performances over the years remain some of the happiest memories of my life. Singing again after twenty-five years brought back all the joy and exhilaration I remembered as a young woman. I know I carry that around with me on a daily basis.

Fast forward about ten years: I remember walking along the beach in the mid-eighties with various friends, discussing with them my dreams of leaving the corporate world and starting my own business. I even had the name Renaissance picked out long before I made the leap. Ironically, our friendships either ended sadly or just faded away due to mutual disinterest, but these friends were significant people in my life for exactly the amount of time they were supposed to be there. Those friends are Kelly and Leslie, the latter of whom first suggested I write a book back in 1993. Thank you both for having faith in me and for encouraging my dream.

Speaking of special women, I would be remiss if I didn't acknowledge the *first* and feistiest group of women I ever met: the Rossi women. Nana Rossi, Auntie Angie, Auntie Lydia, who is no longer with us, Auntie Terry, and of course Mom Norma were my original female role models. Nana and Papa Rossi, who emigrated from Italy and spoke little English, raised six children in the Depression and had precious little worldly belongings to their name. Yet Nana especially was a spunky and cantankerous woman who, along with her four daughters, raised families, kept beautiful homes, and all worked outside of the home their entire lives. I simply did not grow up with weak women as my role models.

And speaking of Mom Norma, she is the youngest of the six Rossi children and, at age seventy-three, is still working full-time and actively supporting the goals of her three children in any way she can. A frustrated homemaker in the sixties, she managed to convince my father that her working outside of the house was not a poor reflection on him. By her own admission, domesticity was not her favorite pastime, yet she still kept a lovely and stylish home. Mom raised me to have a strong, independent spirit, and always let me know how capable and competent I was, even as a small child. Sometimes even she can't resist giving me decorating advice, though. I had to chuckle when she told me that the stripes and florals in my beach house really didn't match. I tell her in my best Dragnet voice, "Mom, I'm a trained professional… I can handle it." Much love and thanks to you, Mom, for passing on your spunky "can do" attitude.

And while growing up in my household was hardly harmonious, especially prior to my parents' divorce, both of my parents encouraged all three of their children to be artistic and creative, in whatever form that took. My father Art Pelosi was a successful musician and entrepreneur; I know I inherited those gifts from him. When he passed away in 1993, he left all of his children a generous sum of money; this seed money gave me the security I needed to visualize my dream of leaving my corporate position so that I could follow my heart. Thank you Dad for helping to pave my way.

I also want to thank my siblings, Artie and Gail, for providing their ongoing recollections of our strange and wonderful shared history – full of color, often challenging, and always uniquely ours. After all is said and done, I still believe the glass is half full.

Now to the present day: In September of 2001, I met Paige Stover Hague of Ictus Development. She had such a weird name for her company; I hadn't the vaguest idea what she did for a living. Well, by November, I had not only understood her service offerings, but I hired her to create my website, eventually handle all of my publicity and media relations, and now to publish my book through her brainchild, Acanthus Publishing. If there was ever an example of a Guardian Angel for one's business, mine is Paige. Paige and I still laugh at her blunt but accurate early feedback: "Your logo is horrible, it doesn't represent you in any way… You need a new image." Everything Paige touches turns to gold. Luckily I was able to see the wisdom of her words and my new corporate image was born.

I also wish to send heartfelt thanks to her staff: Mike Black, George

Kasparian, Anthony Manes, and Elizabeth Nollner, who always returned my calls, promptly answered my emails, reassured me that I look younger than my years, and didn't laugh when I told them I wanted my own decorating show on national television. Until that day, I can definitely thank them for gorgeous collateral material, getting me into countless publications, *The Wall Street Journal* for starters, and getting me a guest spot on HGTV's *Designers' Challenge*. Also, a special hug for my Editor Elizabeth Nollner for always helping me find the right words and structure, and lovingly and painstakingly copyediting all 50,000 of my words, about 65 times. This was Beth's first book as well. And I couldn't forget to give a warm squeeze to Anthony Manes, for providing such delightful sketches and a gorgeous design throughout my book.

I owe a heartfelt thank you to Ms. Christine Wojnar, Feng Shui Practitioner extraordinaire. Chris generously availed her time and wisdom to me as I wrote this book, helping to clarify for me the mysteries and subtleties of this ancient art. Chris is more than a consultant, she is a healer.

I couldn't finish my Acknowledgements without thanking a very special person who really jump-started this book: Ms. Joan Collins. Joan is a personal coach with a résumé of past accomplishments that might make some successful human beings feel inadequate. Yet she is a warm, gracious, and almost perpetually positive spirit who I was fortunate to meet in one of my womens' business groups. Joan offered to help me stay on target with my book, and I in turn agreed to help her finish decorating her home office. There's no doubt in my mind that the new valance I designed for her office could never measure up to the gift she gave me of steadfastly expecting my weekly email to report my book's progress. With her support, I wrote this book in six months; prior to that, it was merely a dream. Thank you Coach Joan with hugs and kisses.

And of course, my final thank you goes to the first person I see each morning and the last face I see each night – my husband and self-proclaimed "biggest fan." I met Steven Soby in July of 1996 at a business owners networking group. We palled around as friends for about five months, working out at the gym and attending business functions together, all the while I was strenuously trying to get the Harley-riding man I was dating to fall to love in me. I gave up in October, broken-hearted and dejected. By November, having decided I had had adequate time to lick my wounds and regroup, Steven expressed his desire to deepen our relationship and become more than friends. After about an hour of my giving him countless rationalizations as to why it probably wouldn't work, we went to a movie – and I don't think we have been apart since.

Let me say that having witnessed many unhappy marriages as a young girl, and having myself divorced at age thirty-two, I frankly held out little hope for the concept of true and enduring love. Yet, to my surprise and delight, by age thirty-seven, I had met the man with whom I'd chose to walk through life. Steven is not only the consummate fan – he is one of my wisest teachers. A few years ago, Leslie, the friend I mentioned earlier, gave us both a personality assessment (Myers Briggs, perhaps?). She told us with an expression of almost maternal gratefulness, "You're polar opposites of each other, but each of you is striving to become more like the other. This is why your relationship is so lovely." That seems to sum up the magic of Steven and me.

Steven introduced me to Buddhism and the fine art of letting go, which still remains a challenge to this recovering Type-A personality. He lifts me up when I'm nagged by feelings of self-doubt and never grows tired of my company, nor I his. So as the song says, "I have all that I could want, and I could not ask for more." Thank you, my love; as we said in our wedding vows, the best is yet to be.

And another heartfelt thanks to all the beautiful kitties who were so patient to pose for pictures! Clockwise from top left: Lilly, Henley, Squiggles, Daisy, Goose, Winston, and Zachary.

In loving memory of Winston, Zachary, and Quentin, who isn't pictured here, but is very much in our hearts.

Appendix

Measurements Chart

Room: _____

Qty.	Windows	Length	Width	Notes
	Style:			
	Style:			
	Style:			

Qty.	Doors	Length	Width	Notes
	Style:			
	Style:			
	Style:			

Qty.	Moldings	Length	Width	Depth
	Style:			
	Style:			
	Style:			

Qty.	Fireplace	Height	Width	Depth
	Mantel:			
	Hearth:			

Qty.	HVAC	Height	Width	Depth
	A/C			
	Heat			

Extra Notes

Measurements Chart

Room: *Living Room*

Qty.	**Windows**	Length	Width	Notes
2	Style: *Picture*	68"	36"	*front of house*
2	Style: *Double-hung*	68"	24"	*side of fireplace*
	Style:			

Qty.	**Doors**	Length	Width	Notes
1	Style: *Open arch*	63"	35"	*from hallway*
1	Style: *Closet door*	63"	32"	*louvered*
1	Style: *French doors*	63"	60"	*to dining room*

Qty.	**Moldings**	Length	Width	Depth
	Style: *Crown molding*		7"	3/4"
	Style: *Baseboard*		5"	1/2"
	Style:			

Qty.	**Fireplace**	Height	Width	Depth
	Mantel: *Wood*	49"	72"	12"
	Hearth: *Brick*	45"	59"	21" *(step 6" high)*

Qty.	**HVAC**	Height	Width	Depth
	A/C	*N/A*		
	Heat	24"	30"	10"

Extra Notes

Radiator under picture window — no room for anything else

Mine

My absolute favorites...	I can live with...	I can't tolerate...

Our common style includes...

Yours

My absolute favorites...	I can live with...	I can't tolerate...

Our common style includes...

STYLE GUIDE

Here are just a few popular styles and the items that exemplify them.

RETRO
- Vintage fabrics
- Chrome kitchen table and chairs with iridescent vinyl seat coverings
- Classic car motif for any accessories
- Canisters, cookie jars, sugar bowls and creamers, pitchers from the fifties
- Fiestaware
- Bakelite serving pieces
- Printed glassware from the fifties
- Black and white square linoleum tiles
- Colors: red, periwinkle blue, bright sky blue, black and white, cotton candy pink, fifties aqua

ECLECTIC
- A mix of styles and genres unified with fabrics and colors
- Animal patterns on rugs, pillows, and linens
- Glittery chandeliers
- Traditional sofa mixed with contemporary coffee table
- Neo-Classical motif accessories, such as busts, statuettes, and sconces
- Oriental accents such as four-panel divider screen or Tansu chest
- Mid-century modern lamps
- Baroque-era lamps with feathers and beads
- Colors: can be bold and bright or soft and neutral

COUNTRY

- **Baskets**
- **Earthenware crocks and pitchers**
- **Old dolls and carved wood figurines**
- **Roosters**
- **Watering cans**
- **Lace**
- **Dried flowers**
- **Checkerboard, gingham, and small floral fabrics**
- **Oak furniture**
- **Jelly cabinets**
- **Antique iceboxes**
- **Hoosier cabinets**
- **Distressed finishes**
- **Colors: earth tones, burgundy, brown, umber, forest green**

"ZEN"/EASTERN

- **Water fountains**
- **Low straight-lined furnishings**
- **Embroidered pillows and throws**
- **Frosted candle cups**
- **Wall hangings with Chinese symbols**
- **Silk floor pillows**
- **Orchids**
- **Wooden trays in satin or matte finish**
- **Simple vases in organic shapes**
- **Sheer drapery panels in cotton or linen**
- **Tumbled stones**
- **Asian statues**
- **Colors: soft and muted lavender, cappuccino, celadon green, robin's egg blue, light olive**

RESOURCES

Here are some great websites for you to check out in your journey toward a more beautiful and functional home!

CANDLES

Candles by K, *www.CandlesbyK.com*

Bath & Body Works, *www.bathandbodyworks.com*

Diptyque Candles, *www.diptyque.tm.fr*

Jo Malone, *www.jomalone.com*

Yankee Candle Company, *www.yankeecandle.com*

CHARITIES

The Salvation Army, *www.salvationarmyusa.org*

Big Brothers Big Sisters of America, *www.bbbs.org*

Father Bill's Place, *www.fatherbillsplace.org*

Morgan Memorial Goodwill Industries, *www.goodwillmass.org*

The Second Step, *www.thesecondstep.org*

FABRIC SOURCES

Country Curtains, *www.countrycurtains.com*

Fashion Fabrics Club On-Line, *www.fashionfabricsclub.com*

Waverly Fabrics, *www.waverly.com*

Zoffany Fabrics, *www.Zoffany.co.uk*

HOME DÉCOR

Ballard Design Catalog, *www.BallardDesigns.com*

The Bombay Company, *www.bombayco.com*

Design Toscano Catalog, *www.DesignToscano.com*

Domestications Catalog, *www.Domestications.com*

Down Inc., *www.buychoice.com*

Everything Nautical Catalog, *www.EverythingNautical.com*

Eddie Bauer Home Catalog, *www.eddiebauerhome.com*

Home Decorators Catalog, *www.homedecorators.com*

Horchow Catalog, *www.horchow.com*

IKEA, *www.IKEA.com*

Levenger Catalog, *www.Levenger.com*

Mitchell Gold Company, *www.mitchellgold.com*

Neiman Marcus, *www.NeimanMarcus.com*

PBteen, *www.pbteen.com*

Pier One Imports, *www.peir1.com*

Pottery Barn, *www.potterybarn.com*

Pottery Barn Kids, *www.potterybarnkids.com*

Restoration Hardware, *www.RestorationHardware.com*

Sauder Furniture, *www.sauder.com*

Sears Department Stores, *www.sears.com*

Spiegel Catalog, *www.spiegel.com*

Storehouse Catalog, **www.storehouse.com**

Sure Fit Slipcovers Catalog, **www.surefit.com**

HomeGoods, **www.homegoods.com**

Victorian Trading Co., **www.victoriantradingco.com**

West Elm Catalog, **www.westelm.com**

HOME IMPROVEMENT

AJ Prindel & Company, **www.ajprindle.com**

Arm & Hammer Products, **www.armandhammer.com**

The Home Depot, **www.homedepot.com**

Improvements Catalog, **www.ImprovementsCatalog.com**

Krylon Paints, **www.krylon.com**

Lowe's Home Improvement Warehouse, **www.Lowes.com**

Solutions Catalog, **www.SolutionsCatalog.com**

Zinsser Paint Products, **www.zinsser.com**

ORGANIZATION

Lillian Vernon Catalog, **www.lillianvernon.com**

The Container Store, **www.thecontainerstore.com**

Hold Everything, **www.holdeverything.com**

National Organization of Professional Organizers, **www.napo.net**

OUTDOORS

Frontgate, *www.frontgate.com*

Gardener's Eden, *www.gardenerseden.com*

Rubbermaid Home Products, *www.rubbermaid.com*

Smith & Hawkin, *www.smith-hawken.com*

PERSONAL GROWTH

Joan Collins, Professional and Personal Coach, *www.joancollinscoach.com*

PET FURNITURE & ACCESSORIES

Petsnap, *www.petsnap.com*

Post Modern Pets, *www.postmodernpets.com*

WINDOW COVERINGS

Comfortex Window Fashions, *www.comfortex.com*

Hunter Douglas Window Coverings, *www.hunterdouglas.com*

Kensington Blinds, *www.kensingtonblinds.com*

Smith + Noble, *www.smithnoble.com*

SUGGESTED READING

Ashwell, Rachel. *Shabby Chic*. New York: HarperCollins Publishers, 1996.

Breathnach, Sarah Ban. *Simple Abundance*. New York: Time Warner, 1995.

Collins, Terah Kathryn. *Home Design with Feng Shui*, A-Z. California: Hay House, 1999.

Daniels, Alison. *Feng Shui for You and Your Cat*. New York: Watson-Guptill Publications, 2000.

Gawain, Shatke. *Living In the Light*. New York: Bantam Publishing, 1993.

Gold, Taro. *Living Wabi-Sabi*, Missouri: Andrews McMeel Publishing, 2004.

Kimball, Cheryl. *The Everything Home Decorating Book*. Massachusetts: Adams Media Corp., 2003.

Koren, Leonard. *Wabi-Sabi for Artists, Designers, Poets, and Philosophers*. Berkeley: Stone Bridge Press, 1994.

Lawrence, Robin Griggs. *The Wabi-Sabi House*. New York: Clarkson Potter, 2004.

Lazenby, Gina. *The Feng Shui House Book*. New York: Watson-Guptill Publications, 1998.

Lennon, Robin. *Home Design from the Inside Out*. New York: Penguin Group, 1997.

Linn, Denise. *Sacred Space*. New York: Ballantine Books, 1995.

Pollack, Jane. *Sole Proprietor*. California: The Crossing Press, 2001.

Popcorn, Faith. *The Popcorn Report*. New York: HarperCollins Publishers, 1992.

Richardson, Cheryl. *Take Time For Your Life*. New York: Broadway Books, 1998.

Richardson, Cheryl. *Life Makeovers*. New York: Broadway Books, 2000.

Richardson, Cheryl. *Stand Up For Your Life*. New York: Free Press, 2002.

Richardson, Cheryl. *The Unmistakable Touch of Grace*. New York: Free Press, 2005.

INDEX

ABOUT THE AUTHOR

Jayne M. Pelosi

Jayne has always had a flair for the dramatic and a passion for all that is beautiful – particularly interior spaces. She launched Renaissance Interior Design from her home in Massachusetts in 1993, following a much-acclaimed career in sales management in the communications industry. During her twelve years as principal in her own firm she has transformed Boston condominiums, vacation homes on the Cape, new construction for growing families in the suburbs, and turn-of-the-century bungalows for subway commuters.

Jayne graduated from Boston University Summa Cum Laude with Distinction in Psychology, which accounts, at least in part, for her wonderful way with people and her fabulous listening skills. Jayne studied design at the Sheffield School of Interior Design, based in New York City, but considers herself predominantly self-taught. Her approach to the design process is to determine her client's vision for their home and translate that into a reality, integrating the client's favorite things with thoughtfully chosen acquisitions.

Jayne's home was featured in the 2004 Spring House Tour for her town and she has contributed to several national publications, including *Today's Home – Bedrooms and Baths* and *Today's Home – 101 Do-It-Yourself Decorating Projects*. She has also been featured in *The Wall Street Journal, The Boston Globe, The Boston Herald*, and many local publications. She was spotlighted on NBC's morning magazine program "Real Life" and was also featured in an episode of HGTV's (Home and Garden Television) hit interior design show *Designers' Challenge*. She writes a monthly column for the national publication *The Homesteader* and is a regular contributor to HGTV.com and *HGTV Decorating*, the online newsletter for Home and Garden Television Network.

She is active in New England Women's Business Owners (NEWBO) and is currently serving as the President of the South Shore Women's Business Network (SSWBN). She is also a member of the local Business Association and Garden Club. When not busily decorating, Jayne can be found singing first Soprano with the Snug Harbor Community Chorus, or collecting shells at her West Dennis beach house on 'ole Cape Cod. Her favorite pastime is spending time with her husband Steven Soby and their two felines Lilly and Henley.

THE PHOTOGRAPHER

Kelli Ruggere

Kelli Ruggere has been behind a camera lens since she was six years old. Although she was quite happy to play with inexpensive instamatic cameras, her parents recognized her burgeoning talent and bought her a Pentax K1000 camera for her twelfth birthday. So inspired by the new equipment, Kelli wrote an essay in seventh grade proclaiming to the world that when she grew up, she was going to be a photographer.

Keeping her word and becoming a professional photographer has been the fulfillment of Kelli's lifelong dream. Kelli graduated from the Rhode Island School of Photography and has been in business for herself for fifteen years. Kelli's unique gift for mastering the application of both natural and artificial lighting has made her a sought-after photographer by interior designers, contractors, and builders all over New England.

Shooting fully in digital format, Kelli is able to immediately prepare all images and save them to a disc, which she can promptly deliver to her clients in record time. She may also deliver her finished product as full color prints upon request. Kelli is as adept at shooting humble subjects as she is shooting exquisite and elaborate interiors. "Anything can be photographed beautifully as long as you control the lighting," is Kelli's mantra. She is currently under contract shooting jewelry and gift items for the Potpourri Group Inc., one of the nation's leading catalogue companies. In addition, she shoots jewelry for the popular BJ's Wholesale Club Inc.

Kelli is a blissful newlywed and enjoys spending her quiet time with her husband John and two beloved Belgian Malinois, Ysi and Max. She lives in what she describes as bucolic Western Massachusetts.

JAYNE'S DESIGN SERVICES

DESIGN MENTOR

Ever wanted to consult a professional about a design issue in your house, but didn't require their complete services? Are you considering purchasing an item for your home but wish you could get the professional "thumbs up" before making a costly mistake? Can you imagine the comfort, convenience, and cost savings of receiving design coaching over the telephone?

Look no further! "Design Mentor" can help you determine what colors, styles, or textures will look best in your house, and offer guidance as you create and execute your very own design plans.

Just imagine: you can send us a picture of any room in your home and we will suggest stylish furnishings, fabrics, and accessories to help create the room of your dreams. Or, for you do-it-yourself designers out there, send us a picture of a room you're in the process of remaking on your own, and we'll provide objective professional feedback on your work.

DESIGN FACELIFT

Our "Design Facelift" provides you with a complete plan for transforming the look and feel of your entire house. Depending on your preference, we can implement the design changes ourselves, or leave the legwork and labor up to you.

We address all decorating aspects of your rooms, from the overall décor theme to the functionality of the space; from accessories and artwork to furniture arrangement and window treatments. We can help you create the room of your dreams!

STAGING

Looking to sell your house? Renaissance Interior Design can help increase the selling price by providing affordable and easy-to-implement design suggestions that will accent your home's best features. We will rearrange furniture, declutter rooms, and recommend sub-contractors, if necessary. With a few (usually) simple and inexpensive alterations to your home's interior design, we can help take out some of the pain of selling your home.

FENG SHUI

• Is your life moving in the direction you want?
• Are you happy in your relationships?
• Is your professional life as prosperous as it could be?
• Do you feel balance in your physical and mental health?
• Is all of your space meeting your needs?

If you answered "No" to any of these questions, perhaps you should consider Feng Shui.

Feng Shui literally means wind and water. It's the ancient Chinese art of placement and maintains that the objects in our environment directly impact all aspects of our lives, including our health, prosperity, and relationships. Feng Shui can reduce stress, create harmony, increase motivation and energy, and improve concentration, just to cite a few of its amazing benefits.

The Pyramid School of Feng Shui focuses on the occupants of a space. It blends ancient tradition with contemporary knowledge of the subliminal effects environments have on our psyches and our health. In the comprehensive interview, we will identify your goals, values, and where you would like to create movement in your life. Our consultant will make Feng Shui recommendations that will help you achieve your goals, and by using space-clearing techniques with the art of dowsing, will identify and clear energetic disturbances. The result: a positive environment in which you can thrive and flourish.